SPINOZA DESCARTES & MAIMONIDES

SPINOZA DESCARTES & MAIMONIDES

By *LEON ROTH, M.A., D.Phil.*

New York
RUSSELL & RUSSELL
1963

FIRST PUBLISHED IN 1924
REISSUED, 1963, BY RUSSELL & RUSSELL, INC.
L. C. CATALOG CARD NO: 63—15176

PRINTED IN THE UNITED STATES OF AMERICA

TO

MY FATHER

PREFACE

IN the following study I have endeavoured to show that (1) in relation to Descartes, Spinoza represents the radical opposition of monism to pluralism; and that (2) this same opposition, in a precisely similar context and with identical presuppositions and consequences, is to be found in a work which on other counts may be shown to have deeply influenced Spinoza, the *Guide for the Perplexed* of Maimonides.

My sincerest thanks are due to Prof. H. H. Joachim for the ungrudging help and careful criticism which he has given me throughout; to Prof. C. C. J. Webb and Prof. A. Wolf for many valuable suggestions; to the Rev. Prof. G. A. Cooke for encouraging my work during my tenure of the James Mew studentship; and to Mr. J. M. Jacobs and Mr. C. B. Oldman for advice on points of style.

The first two chapters were originally published in *Mind* and are here reprinted by kind permission of the Editor.

CONTENTS

I. DESCARTES

II. SPINOZA

III. MAIMONIDES

IV. MAIMONIDES AND SPINOZA

I. DESCARTES

Introductory: Spinoza's use of Descartes

THE problem to the consideration of which I have addressed myself in the two following chapters is that of the nature of the relationship between the philosophies of Spinoza and Descartes. We have on the one hand the pronouncement of a classical monograph that 'Spinoza was never a Cartesian at all';[1] on the other, the well-known and oft-repeated remark of Leibniz that 'Spinoza only cultivated certain seeds of Descartes' philosophy'. In the face of such contradictory opinions it is natural to ask what Spinoza has to tell us on the matter himself. The answer to this question is to be sought for not only and not so much in the few definite statements on the subject which we happen to have from Spinoza, though we know that both in private conversation[2] and in correspondence[3] he spoke slightingly of Descartes, but in an appreciation of the point of view which these statements imply. Modern historians, in the attempt to comprehend 'Cartesianism' as a whole, have been prone to interpret the system of Descartes in the light of its supposed development in Spinoza, and have consequently found it easy, with the help of some additional accommodation, to discover Spinoza in Descartes. The first thesis of this study is that, if the philosophy of Descartes be re-examined in the light of its own logical

[1] Pollock, *Spinoza* (ed. 1912), p. 86.

[2] e. g. 'Credisne, mi Amice, omnia quae Cartesius dixit vera esse?' (Spinoza to Tschirnhaus, ap. Freudenthal, *Lebensgeschichte*, p. 208).

[3] e. g. *Epp.* 2, 43, 81. It will be remembered that he was subjected to much annoyance, if not actual persecution, at the hands of the real Cartesians (*Ep.* 68).

premisses, it will be seen to have resulted, even on Descartes' own admission, in a pluralistic scepticism; that it is this view of Descartes' philosophy which may be shown to underlie all Spinoza's specific criticisms; and that it was precisely this type of thought against which the whole of Spinoza's work was one long and conscious protest.

Now the logic of Descartes is studied, as a rule,[1] from the *Regulae ad directionem Humani Ingenii*, and it has been a matter for some discussion as to how far the opinions of this early work persist in or exercised influence over, the mature thought of the *Meditations*.[2] It happens, however, that the *Regulae*, and with it the *Recherche de la Vérité*, was not published in any form till after Spinoza's death, and must therefore from the point of view of the present inquiry be completely disregarded. If we wish to form a conception of the Cartesian logic as it presented itself to Spinoza, we must turn to the *Discourse on Method*, the *Meditations* with the *Objections* and *Replies*, the *Principles of Philosophy*, the *Passions of the Soul*, and the *Letters*, all of which we know to have been possessed, and used, by Spinoza.[3] From a study of these works, a certain view of the Cartesian logic results. Whether it be allowed to be the only possible view or no,

[1] e. g. by Norman Kemp Smith in his *Studies in the Cartesian Philosophy*; cf. Höffding, *History of Modern Philosophy*, p. 510, n. 43 (E.T.).

[2] Cf. the articles of Berthet and Natorp in the Descartes number of the *Revue de Métaphysique et de Morale* (1896).

[3] *Lebensgeschichte*, p. 161 (the library list), nos. 10, 20, 21, 24, 25. For direct quotations, cf. e. g. *Short Treatise*, I, cap. 7 end (from *Replies to Objections*); *Princ. Phil. Cart.* I, Proleg. iii (from *Principia*, *Meditations*, and *Replies to Objections*); *Ethics*, V, pref. (from *Passions of the Soul*); *Princ. Phil. Cart.* II. 6 sch. end (from the *Letters*).

References to the works of Descartes, except the *Letters*, have been given by the page and line of Adam and Tannery's edition; to the *Letters*, by the pages of the Latin edition (Amsterdam, 1668), which, like the Dutch version possessed by Spinoza, comprises Clerselier's first and second volumes only. The English is, as a rule, that of Haldane and Ross (Cambridge, 1911–12).

evidence will be advanced later to suggest that this was the logic which was understood by Spinoza to be the Cartesian, and which, as Cartesian, was specifically combated by him throughout his philosophical career.

§ 1. *The New Method: its Character and Antecedents*

The *Discourse on Method* commences with an account of Descartes' search for truth. From the fact that although 'good sense' is common to all, yet opinions on every important question are different, he concluded that the existence of these differences, apparent particularly between and within the various systems of philosophy, must be due to faults in method. Even in the sphere which commanded most agreement and where demonstration had been achieved, that of mathematics, the methods commonly employed were too confused and fatiguing to be taken as a model. It was necessary, therefore, first to disengage the essential procedure of the purest types of mathematics, and then to take over the result for application to all the sciences alike. The characteristics of the logic so achieved might be expected to be the same as those of geometry and algebra—simplicity of premiss; universality of application; and inevitableness of conclusion.

This, the thought of the first two parts of the *Discourse* is repeated generally throughout Descartes' works. He was impressed by two outstanding facts, the certainty and comprehensiveness of mathematical knowledge and the uncertainty and sterility of non-mathematical knowledge. Now this recognition of the peculiar character of mathematical knowledge is not original to Descartes. It is common to most of the great figures of the Renaissance, who, in their struggle against what they considered to be the arid logic of the Schoolmen, turned their eyes towards mathematics as the one science through which the mind of man 'could find new light in the darkness of the corporeal world ; enlarge its powers so as to embrace the whole universe ; and win for itself a triumphant peace '.[1] And not only the admiration for mathematics as a liberating science, but also the conception of the employment of its method in the other sciences, is older than Descartes. He himself remarks that ' it is not novel, since there is nothing more ancient than the truth ' ; [2] and in an interesting letter to Mersenne [3] declares that it was this, and this only, of which he approved in the work of Galileo. But whether or no Descartes originated the high esteem in which the mathematical method was held, it was without doubt the conception which influenced him most profoundly in the development of his philosophy.

The primary fault of the Aristotelian logic, then (to return to Descartes' criticism), at least as it had been developed in the schools, was that, at its best, it was a dialectic useful for expository purposes only, and, at its worst, a lip repetition of dubious and useless formulae.[4] It was in fact an instrument rather for classification than for fresh discovery, and that classification within traditional boundaries only. But the aim of any logic should be precisely to point the way to fresh discovery ; and the unsatisfactoriness of Aristotelian principles could not be more clearly demonstrated than by the fact that they had produced no new truths.[5] The justification of the new method proposed in the *Discourse,* therefore, was the appended collection of special scientific treatises ; the justification of the *Principia,* its scientific presentation of the

[1] See generally Cassirer, *Erkenntnisproblem* (Berlin, 1906), vol. i. The quotation is the substance of an eloquent passage of Ramus (ib., p. 132).

[2] *Med. Ep.* (p. 3, ll. 24–5).

[3] *Ep.* II, xci, pp. 276 and 281.

[4] *Author's Letter* prefaced to the French edition of the *Principia,* p. 13, l. 24 f.

[5] *Author's Letter,* p. 18, l. 29 f. ; *Ep. ad P. Dinet,* p. 579, l. 30 f. ; *Ep. ad Voetium,* p. 26, l. 1 f.

phenomena of Nature as a whole. The new logic is the instrument for the construction of a 'universal science',[1] 'the roots of which are metaphysics; the trunk physics; the branches all the other sciences.'[2] Just as in Geometry even the propositions of Archimedes are not obscure if we give patient attention to the preceding demonstrations, so in the whole of Nature there is no question too remote for the grasp, or too deep for the understanding, of the ordinary man.[3]

This comparison of the difficulties of physical investigations with those of Geometry strikes the note which dominates Cartesian logic, and it is the peculiar value of the narrative of the *Discourse* that it shows that the mathematical method detailed in the *Regulae* is as an historical fact the real starting-point for the thought of the *Meditations*. The rules of the second *Discourse* emphasize the twofold necessity of analysing a problem into its constituent smaller problems and then arranging these constituents in some definite order; while the fourth and the fifth *Discourses* are devoted to the search for principles on which metaphysics and physics may be based, principles which were afterwards to be employed in the *Meditations* and *Principia*. The doctrines of 'simple ideas' and 'simple natures' are in fact only different applications to the spheres of logic and physics of what appeared to Descartes to be the starting-point of mathematics. The long chains of 'reasonings'[4] wherewith mathematicians build out into the unknown must be imitated in the realms of physics. As geometry starts with principles, so physics must start with principles; as geometry moves away from its principles, so the new physics will move away from its principles. Now the

[1] *Ep.* II, cxi, p. 378.

[2] *Author's Letter*, p. 14, ll. 24–7.

[3] e. g. *Ep.* I, cx, p. 350. The comparison of metaphysical with geometrical propositions is in *Med. Ep.*, p. 4, l. 15 f.

[4] 'Raisons', *Disc.* II, p. 19, l. 6 f.

word 'principle' may be used in many senses.[1] One may conceive of a principle as a whole out of which everything else may be as an actual fact deduced (or rather educed), much in the same way as out of certain puzzle boxes a long series of progressively smaller boxes may be successively taken. Or one may conceive of it as an abstract formula, to which everything may be expected to conform—an example is the principle of contradiction. Or finally one may conceive of it as an instrument to be actually used in the process of discovery, e. g. the principle of the mechanical interpretation of nature which has proved so fruitful in physical investigations. It was in this last sense that Descartes specifically understood the word, and for the reason that it was only as an instrument of discovery that he put any value upon 'principles' at all; and from the point of view of fresh discovery it was no use postulating as a principle what one aimed at discovering, or putting one's faith in an abstract formula which would be useful only (if at all) in determining the abstract characteristics of the discovery when made. As opposed to the traditional logic, therefore, which confined itself to the enunciation of universal 'truths' and discovered nothing new, the new logic was to use the touchstone of the principles in order to move from one particular which was known to another particular which was unknown. The 'deduction', to use Descartes' word,[2] though it is not deduction in the usual sense, was to be unilateral, proceeding from one point, previously determined, to the next, and so on and on until some hitherto unknown result had been achieved. The whole emphasis is on the novelty [3] of the various links as they are being forged. True,

[1] *Ep.* I, cxviii, p. 379.

[2] e. g. *Disc.* II, p. 19, l. 14, and repeatedly in *Author's Letter*, e. g. p. 9, l. 20; p. 10, ll. 14, 18; p. 20, ll. 7–8, 22.

[3] . . . ce soit d'eux [=les principes] que dépende la connaissance des autres choses, en sorte qu'ils puissent être connus sans elles, mais non pas reciproquement elles sans eux . . . *Author's Letter*, p. 2, ll. 23–5.

the principles on which we work must be so fundamental as not to depend for their certainty on any deduction made from them; but the aim of the method is to show how the deductions, each one of which is to be manifest by itself, may be drawn one after another from the principles. The first satisfaction gained from the method, we are told in the *Author's Letter* prefixed to the French version of the *Principia* in which a general account is given of the aim and method of the new logic, is the actual discovery of new truths; and the last, the acquiring of the general habit of discovery, so that 'passing little by little from one to the other, we may acquire in time a perfect knowledge of the whole of philosophy and ascend to the highest degree of wisdom'.[1]

It is obvious that in this account of the unilateral as the ideal type of reasoning three main difficulties disengage themselves. The first relates to the selection of any one point as a starting-point; the second to the movement from any one point to another; the third to the general character of the whole process as it eventuates in the discoveries of science. Since in fact the 'chain of reasoning' is made up of distinct and discrete elements, it is necessary to inquire how the discrete elements may be said to become a 'chain' at all. The three problems, those of the criterion, the movement, and the ground or guarantee, call for separate metaphysical elucidation.

§ 2. *The First Problem of the Method: the Criterion*

(*a*) *Its nature.* To resolve the first problem, that of the criterion of the individual truth, Descartes adopts frankly a theory of intuition. It is to an intuition that we owe our first premiss, an intuition behind which we cannot go. Of the nature of the intuition little is told us.[2] It is the power

[1] *Author's Letter*, p. 17, l. 26 to p. 18, l. 20; cf. *Principia*, iv, 199.
[2] The word intuition itself is almost confined to the *Regulae* (e. g. Rule XI), but cf. e. g. *Resp.* II, p. 140, l. 23 ('rem per se notam simplici

to recognize an idea as clear and distinct, but clearness and distinctness are irreducible qualities definable only in terms of themselves.[1] It is evidently to be identified with the 'good sense' with which the *Discourse* opens, or the appeal to 'natural reason in its purity' with which it closes. It is the 'light given by God' to man wherewith to 'distinguish truth and error'; the 'natural light' which assures us that 'there must be at least as much reality in the cause as in the effect'; the 'natural knowledge' which tells us that 'the mind is distinct from the body'.[2] A discussion on this last point with a doctor of the Sorbonne elicited from Descartes a clearer statement of one side of the criterion of clarity and distinctness by which the intuition recognizes truths. After laying down the general principle that 'there must be in things everything contained in the idea of those things', that is to say that the world of ideas is complete in itself and hence autonomous and not subject to the interference of objects; he says that the only way to know whether an idea is complete in itself is to examine its origin and see whether inadvertently a transference has taken place or no, by an 'abstraction of the intellect', not from another object but from another idea. He then goes on: 'the idea of extended and figured substance

mentis intuitu'), and *Ep.* I, ciii, p. 338 ('Clarissima, et, si liceat ita loqui, intuitiva, cognitio). The possibility and nature of intuitional knowledge ('connaissance intuitive') is discussed in a letter to Mersenne in the third volume of the Letters (Angot, Paris, 1667, p. 638 f.), where its definition as 'une illustration de l'esprit, par laquelle il voit en la lumière de Dieu les choses qu'il lui plaît lui découvrir, par une impression directe de la clarté divine sur notre entendement, qui en cela n'est point considéré comme Agent, mais seulement comme recevant les rayons de la Divinité' points clearly to its origin in Augustinian Neo-Platonism.

[1] *Princ.* I. 45.

[2] 'Bon sens' (*Disc.* I, p. 1 : 17); 'raison naturelle toute pure' (*Disc.* VI, p. 77 : 28); 'quelque lumière' (*Disc.* III, p. 27 : 24); 'lumen naturale' (*Med.*, p. 40 : 21); 'naturalis cognitio' (*Resp.* II, p. 153 : 11). The Cartesian doctrine of mind is considered below, p. 19, n. 3.

is complete because I can conceive of it alone and by itself and deny of it all other things of which I have ideas. Now it seems to me to be perfectly clear that the idea which I have of thinking substance is complete in this manner, and that there is no idea in my mind which precedes it or which is so joined with it that I cannot conceive them rightly while denying one of the other.' From this clear statement,[1] the significance of which only becomes apparent later, though it is after all no more than a reaffirmation of the first premiss, we see that the very essence of the true idea is its discreteness. If an idea is not completely self-contained, i. e. if it cannot be understood by itself apart from reference to any other, it is not, in the Cartesian sense, distinct, and therefore is not, by the Cartesian standard, true.

(*b*) *Its source.* It is legitimate to ask how we arrive at the criterion of clarity and distinctness at all. Descartes has his answer ready. In the process of the universal doubt man is forced to acknowledge the fact of his own existence as indubitable. An examination of this primary fact shows that it is characterized by clarity and distinctness. Clarity and distinctness therefore may be adopted as the test of the truth of any other idea. The criterion of clarity and distinctness rests on the examination of the characteristics of the knowledge of the self and is hence posterior to it. Not that the validity of all clear and distinct ideas depends on the idea of the self in the sense that they all may be deduced from it in one way or another; but the choice of the criterion of clarity and distinctness depends upon the fact that clarity and distinctness are the characteristic marks of the type of all true ideas, the idea of the self.[2]

The argument aims at finding a metaphysical basis for

[1] *Ep.* I, cv, pp. 341–2.

[2] *Disc.* IV, p. 33: 16 f.; *Med.* III, p. 35: 7 f.; *Med.* IV, p. 58: 25 f.

the criterion of truth, but it would seem to rest on a logical inversion. The method of investigation with which Descartes sets out is the mathematical method, that is, the method characterized by its employment of the criterion of clarity and distinctness. With this method he searches for a starting-point for thought and proceeds to doubt everything about which he can doubt, that is to say, everything which is not perfectly clear and distinct. Having at last achieved an idea about which he cannot doubt, he examines its nature and notes that it is clear and distinct, and then adopts the clarity and distinctness of an idea as the universal criterion of logical validity. But seeing that in his very search for a starting-point it was precisely clarity and distinctness for which he looked, it is not remarkable that he should discover these characteristics in the starting-point which he finally found. From the point of view therefore of the criterion of clarity and distinctness the ' thinking self ' is only one among many other self-evident truths or intuitions and cannot be considered to be their foundation.[1]

Descartes himself, when pressed on the subject of the argument which proved the existence of the self, replied in substance that there was no argument about it at all but that the recognition of the existence of the self was an immediate intuition.[2] This position in itself is of course sound, but it has important consequences for the further development of the logic. If we allow the unquestionable validity of one intuition it is difficult to disallow (and Descartes himself never disallowed) the validity of others.[3] But if so, it is not the thinking self which is the premiss and foundation of our knowledge but the ' lumen naturale ' with its many and various intuitions. And in fact the criterion of truth which far from being derived from,

[1] For the self as only one of many simple ideas see e. g. *Resp.* II, p. 145 : 22 f.

[2] *Resp.* II, p. 140 : 18 f.

[3] See *Princ.* I. 7, 10, 13, and 49.

is presupposed in, the argument for the existence of the thinking self, springs out of the very nature of the 'lumen naturale'.[1]

§ 3. *The Second Problem of the Method: the Movement*

Having firmly grasped the character and the fundamental importance of the clear and distinct idea and the validity of the criterion of clarity and distinctness, we must turn to consider the nature of the movement from one clear and distinct idea to another. Now the impetus for the movement cannot come from the external object, or objects; because, as we have seen, the world of ideas is autonomous, reflecting, or corresponding with, not interacting with, the world of objects.[2] Nor can the source of movement lie in the mind itself, because the mind is the same as, and cannot be distinguished from, ideas; and since the ideas to be true must be discrete, there cannot be a unitary, much less an active, mind at all.[3] The

[1] 'Perspicuitas intellectus a natura indita' (Postulate 3 of Append. to *Resp.* II, p. 163, l. 3). 'Quod intelligam quid sit res, quid sit veritas, quid sit cogitatio, haec non aliunde habere videor quam *ab ipsamet mea natura* . . . (*Med.* III, p. 38: 1 f.). 'Quod ad . . . Doctorem illum attinet qui dicit posse nos dubitare utrum cogitemus, non minus quam de quavis alia re, in *lumen naturale* tam graviter impingit ut mihi persuadeam neminem in eius sententia futurum qui ad verba eius attendet.' (*Ep.* II, liv, pp. 208–9.)

[2] Above, p. 16.

[3] 'Nullam aliam differentiam statuo inter animam et eius ideas quam inter frustum cerae et diversas figuras quarum frustum illud capax est; et quemadmodum diversas figuras recipere, non est in cera actio proprie sed passio: ita mihi videtur passio esse etiam in anima, quod hanc vel illam ideam recipiat, et praeter volitiones nullas esse ipsius actiones existimo.' (*Ep.* I, cxv, p. 369.)

Descartes is not too consistent on this point. In the letter to Voetius, quoted on p. 23, note, he uses the Socratic argument to prove the existence of a native knowledge in the mind, and in his notes against the first article of Regius' program claims as his original contribution the definition of the mind as the 'faculty of thinking' and the 'inward source' of thought. The fuller development of the logic however shows that this strand is not the central one in Descartes, and that the

central problem of the Cartesian logic, therefore, is, how can we, assuming a theory which gives us only discrete thoughts, arrive at the whole of truth? If there are no real connexions between ideas, in fact, how can we speak of truth at all? Descartes was fully aware of the importance of this question and attempted to meet it by shifting the centre of his system away from the doubting self and clear and distinct perceptions altogether, and making it the idea of God.

The idea of God as (a) primary starting-point. Now it is clear that the idea of God cannot be substituted for the thinking self as primary starting-point. The Cartesian arguments for the existence of God are variously stated, even in succeeding paragraphs, but correspond to two broad types. The first is from the idea in our minds of perfection to the existence outside our minds of a perfect being as a cause of the idea within us. The second is from the idea of God as existing to the fact of God as existing.[1] Both exhibit the same fundamental characteristic of starting out from the self. It is the self which is conscious of imperfection and the self which possesses the idea of perfection. It is therefore the self and

discretion which is noted by N. K. Smith as being the characteristic of the *Regulae* runs through the whole of Descartes' work. If we once admit that the intellections and memory of man depend on the conservation of God (below, e. g. p. 27, n. 1), then there can be no such thing as a judgement at all and the whole doctrine of intuitive axioms falls to the ground.

It is worthy of note that the 'continuous and uninterrupted act of thought' which 'runs over the whole of a number of simple truths' and 'infers one thing from another', of the *Regulae*, does not reappear in the later works. Instead we have the direct movement from the mind to God and from God to things and propositions, to be described later (§§ 3–4). The difference is well marked in a comparison of e. g. *Reg.* XI with the summary of the method in *Princ.* I. 75.

[1] 'Duae tantum sunt viae per quas possit probari Deum esse, una nempe per effectus et altera per ipsam eius essentiam sive naturam.' (*Resp.* I, p. 120 : 9 f.) The two arguments are detailed most clearly in *Ep.* I. xcix (=Notes against a Programme), p. 328, and in the geometrical appendix to the second set of Replies.

the self alone which we can make our starting-point in thinking.[1]

(*b*) *Secondary starting-point.* If the idea of God cannot be the primary, can it be the essential secondary, premiss in the system of knowledge? An examination of Descartes' thought shows that the nerve of his argument is that the only possible step forward from the recognition of the existence of the self is the recognition of the existence of God, and that therefore the mediation [2] of the idea of God is essential if we would proceed beyond the self to an investigation of the external world.[3] To sustain such a position it would be necessary to prove that the recognition of the doubting self is the sole logical prius in knowledge, and that the essential and only possible complement to the recognition of the doubting self is the recognition of the existence of God. If this could be shown it would follow that it is only through the idea of God that we can approach the sciences and that therefore a denial of the existence of God involves the invalidity of the sciences.

Both of these premisses however are, on Cartesian principles, invalid. That, starting from the self, we can only proceed to the existence of God and nothing else, is, it is true, constantly suggested by Descartes, who implies, though he does not prove,

[1] 'Praeterea non tantum quaesivi quae sit causa mei, quatenus sum res cogitans, sed maxime etiam et praecipue quatenus inter ceteras cogitationes *ideam* entis summe perfecti *in me esse animadverto. Ex hoc enim uno* tota vis demonstrationis meae dependet.' (*Resp.* I, p. 107: 20 f.)

[2] 'Dixi vero Scepticos de veritatibus geometricis dubitaturos non fuisse, si Deum ut par est agnovissent, quia, cum istae veritates Geometricae sint admodum perspicuae, non habuissent ullam occasionem de iis dubitandi, si scivissent ea omnia quae perspicue intelliguntur esse vera; hoc autem in sufficienti Dei cognitione continetur atque hoc ipsum est *medium* quod in numerato non habebant.' (*Ep.* II, xvi, p. 91.)

[3] The objective existence of which indeed may only be assumed on the hypothesis of the veracity of God. (*Med.* VI and *Princ.* II, 1.)

by always moving directly from the self to God,[1] that there can conceivably be no other movement ; but he himself notes that in the movement itself many prior conceptions are involved, that of cause, for example,[2] and so acknowledges that the necessity of the movement does not lie within the sole bounds of the original starting-point, the idea of the existing self. But the first premiss is in even worse case. The existence of the doubting self is far from being, as we have noted before, the sole prius in knowledge. It may be true that 'we cannot doubt our existence without existing while we doubt ; and that this is the first knowledge that we obtain when we philosophize in the ordinary way'. Yet we must not forget that philosophy is reflective and that therefore our datum is not the doubting self but the knowledge of the self as doubting. That such knowledge exists depends on the reliability of the primitive intuition of thought, there being a 'contradiction, in conceiving that what thinks does not, at the same time as it thinks, exist'[3] But seeing that from this same primitive intuition there are derived many other axioms which have nothing to do with self or God, it is clear that the sciences may start from these axioms and ignore (from the point of view of logical principle) the existence both of the self and of God.[4]

[1] e. g. *Princ.* I. 75 : '. . . imprimis advertemus *nos* existere, quatenus sumus naturae cogitantis ; et simul etiam et esse *Deum*, et nos ab illo pendere et ex eius attributorum consideratione *ceterarum rerum* veritatem posse indagari . . . '

[2] *Princ.* I. 18 ; *Med.* III, p. 40 : 21 f. ; *Resp.* I, p. 119 : 16 f. ; *Resp.* II, p. 135 : 11 f.

[3] *Princ.* I. 7.

[4] This possibility is brought out clearly in *Princ.* I. 75, where the mind has, '*praeter notiones Dei et mentis nostrae*', ideas of eternal verities and of physical things. The truths of mathematics therefore should not have less validity than the idea of God, as Gassendi remarks (*Obj.*, p. 328 : 2 f.), and as Descartes himself really agrees : 'notandum est eas omnes res, quarum cognitio dicitur nobis esse a natura indita, non ideo a nobis expresse cognosci ; sed tantum tales esse, ut ipsas, absque ullo sensuum experimento, ex proprii ingenii viribus cognoscere possimus. Cuius generis sunt *omnes Geometricae veritates*, non tantum

§ 4. *The Third Problem of the Method: the Ground*

The idea of God therefore can be accepted neither as primary nor as secondary starting-point in the process of thinking. It remains to consider whether in thought as a system it may be shown to hold an essential place. Such a place Descartes sought to find for it by his doctrine of the 'veracity of God'.

The 'veracity of God'. God, he said, being good, is no deceiver, and therefore would not have arranged the world in such a way that our clear ideas should deceive us. Being thus the guarantee of the certainty of our clear ideas, He is the true centre and foundation of the intellectual world.[1]

The circular character of this argument was pointed out to him by his correspondents,[2] and lies of course in the fact that it is from clear ideas in one way or another that we demonstrate the existence of God. The objection of the Theologians and Gassendi therefore that an atheist can be certain that the three angles of a triangle are equal to two right angles,[3] is more pertinent, on Cartesian premisses, than Descartes is disposed to allow. The atheist can be quite sure 'that he is not deceived' in his geometrical reasonings, because he can refer directly to his own clear and distinct perception of the triangle, which cannot but be at least as free from illusion, even assuming the possibility of demoniac influences, as his 'clear and distinct' idea of himself.

Descartes, when confronted with this seemingly illogical

maxime obviae sed etiam reliquae quantumvis abstrusae videantur; atque inde Socrates apud Platonem, puerum quemdam de Geometricis elementis interrogando, sicque efficiendo ut ille puer quasdam veritates ex mente propria erueret, quas prius in ea fuisse non notaverat, reminiscentiam suam probare conabatur. Et *huius etiam generis* est *Dei cognitio*.' (*Ep. ad Voetium*, pp. 166, l. 21–167, l. 8.)

[1] e. g. *Med.* IV; *Princ.* I. 13; I. 30.

[2] e. g. Arnauld (*Obj.* IV, p. 214: 7 f.) and the Theologians (*Obj.* II, p. 124: 29 f.).

[3] *Obj.* II, p. 125: 6 f.; *Obj.* V, p. 328: 7 f.; *Obj.* VI, p. 414: 24 f.

argument by his critics, affirmed that they had misunderstood him. It was not, he says, the original concrete elements in knowledge of which he had spoken, but the 'science' that was derived from them. Inference is unilateral, proceeding from point to point; the mind, by giving patient attention to these points as they are discovered, constructs from them long chains of reasoning, and what we call science is not the intermediate links but the end reached by the whole chain. Now, the validity of our final opinions, Descartes argues, depends on the accuracy with which we remember the chain of our reasonings; unless we can be perfectly sure of our memory, we cannot but suspect our results. We cannot in fact put any reliance on thought as continuous and therefore are forced to call in God as auxiliary. Unless therefore we know that God is not a deceiver, we are liable to suspect that our course of reasoning may have been deliberately perverted; that is to say, we have science no longer, but only opinion or persuasion.[1]

This statement, of course, misses the point of the problem. The problem is not the validity of the end of the chain after it has been fashioned, but that of the fashioning itself of the various discrete elements into the chain. It is little comfort to be assured that our memory has not played us false if we have no reason to trust the original conclusion as we remember it. It is precisely for the reaching of the original conclusion that the necessary means are wanting, and these means are not provided for by the conception of the veracity of God, whether according to the critics' interpretation (when it is a *petitio principii*) or according to Descartes' own (when it burkes the problem altogether). The original crux of the logic therefore remains: how can we build up a whole of knowledge when we have only discrete intuitions with which to build?

[1] *Med.* V; *Resp.* II, p. 146: 14–26; *Resp.* IV, p. 246: 1 f. (where he sums up his reply as 'distinguendo scilicet id quod reipsa clare percipimus ab eo quod recordamur nos antea clare percepisse', &c.); and *Ep.* I, lxxxi, pp. 279–80.

God as conserving cause. Although the doctrine of the veracity of God fails itself to provide a solution to the problem, it yet points out, particularly in its connexion with human memory, the lines of a possible solution. Its application has in fact been too restricted. The idea of God must be introduced, not only for the results, but also for the links and connexions, of an inference. Although, we may say, the discrete elements in knowledge themselves cannot by any manner of means be shown to be dependent on the idea of God, yet their association into a system of science cannot take place without the assistance of the idea of God. In this way what we have seen to be the fundamental problem of the logic would find its solution. God would be conceived of as the 'synthetic unity', as it were, in, or through, which the elements of knowledge are fitted into the great syntheses of elements of knowledge which we know as the sciences. Without God the elements could not cohere, and there could not be such a thing as science. The very possibility of the existence of science therefore depends directly on the hypothesis of God. But God exists: therefore science is a possibility and logic has a justification.

This conception is, from the point of view of the Cartesian logic, of supreme importance. Since the essence of the true idea is its discreteness and distinctness from any other, it follows that any connexions between it and any other idea must be external; and since the essence of science is the perceiving and unification of connexions, some unitary power achieving these connexions must exist. But this power does not reside in the human mind nor can it be allowed to come from the world of objects. We are driven therefore immediately to the transference of the conception of God as a 'conserving cause' in nature to the conception of God as a 'conserving cause' in knowledge.

(*a*) *In nature.* 'The first and most important truth', wrote Descartes to the princess Elizabeth, 'is that a God exists from whom all things depend ; whose perfections are infinite ; whose power immeasurable ; whose decrees infallible.' [1] God is the centre of the Cartesian metaphysic and His characteristic is freedom. The will of God is boundless, omnipotent and infinite, competent to effect all things.[2] Nothing exists which is not directly dependent upon His transcendent power, because the existence of anything independent of Him would imply a limitation of His omnipotence, i. e., a contradiction in His nature.[3] From this it follows immediately that creation was not one final act. Since the characteristic quality of God is will, His characteristic function is creation ; to assert that the work of creation is over and done would be to deny God's present activity, that is, deny His existence. The doctrine of one final creation, then, leads to an atheism which sees the passing away of God with the coming into being of the universe. But since God exists, creation must be continuous. It must be understood, that is, as a constant process of conservation,[4] the act of creation being continually repeated, and that not only in the physical universe, but also in the very

[1] *Ep.* I. vii, p. 16. [2] *Med.* III *passim.*

[3] '. . . nec dubium est si Deus cessaret a suo concursu quin statim omnia quae creavit in nihilum essent abitura, quia antequam creata essent et ipsis concursum suum praeberet nihil erant. . . . Nec Deus ostenderet potentiam suam esse immensam si res tales efficeret ut postea sine ipso esse possent ; sed contra *illam in hoc testaretur esse finitam, quod res semel creatae non amplius ab eo penderent.*' (*Ep.* II, xvi, p. 89.)

'Quantum ad liberum arbitrium si ad nos tantum attendamus fateor non posse nos illud non putare independens ; sed cum ad infinitam Dei potentiam animum advertimus, non possumus non credere omnia ab illo pendere et proinde liberum nostrum arbitrium imperio eius solutum non esse. *Implicat enim contradictionem Deum creasse homines eiusmodi naturae ut voluntatis eorum actiones ab eius voluntate non pendeant* ; quia idem est ac si quis diceret, potentiam eius finitam esse simul ac infinitam ; finitam cum aliquid sit quod ab illo non pendet ; infinitam vero cum potuerit rem hanc independentem creare.' (*Ep.* I, ix, p. 25.)

[4] *Med.* III, p. 48, l. 25 f. ; p. 49, l. 11.

volitions and thoughts of men.[1] This view of creation as conservation involves, of course, an atomistic theory of time. The continuity of the universe depends absolutely on the continuity of the creativeness of God, not on the inherent connexion of the universe with a continuous time. And so Descartes observes : 'The mere duration of our life suffices to prove the existence of God.' And adds : 'We cannot doubt the truth of this demonstration so long as we observe the nature of time, or of the duration of things ; for this is of such a kind that its parts do not depend one upon the other, and never co-exist ; and from the fact that we now are, it does not follow that we shall be a moment afterwards, if some cause—the same that first produced us—does not continue so to produce us, that is, to conserve us . . .'[2]

(*b*) *In knowledge.* The doctrine of conservation, however, which we see to be the direct outcome of the doctrine of the transcendence of God, involves more than a discrete time. The presuppositions of the logic reappear. Everything rests on and in the will of God. There are no necessary connexions between things, because there is no necessity ; nor can we speak of causation in a world in which God is the sole and immediate cause of everything. And just as there are no

[1] '. . . rationes omnes quae Dei existentiam probant, illumque primam esse et immutabilem causam omnium effectuum qui a libero hominum arbitrio non pendent, mihi videri probare *illum etiam esse causam actionum omnium quae a libero arbitrio pendent.* Non enim demonstrari potest quod existat, nisi consideretur ut ens summe perfectum ; non esset autem summe perfectum, siquid in mundo fieri posset quod ab illo omnino non procederet. Verum quidem est sola fide doceri nos quid sit gratia illa per quam Deus ad beatitudinem supernaturalem nos evehit ; sed ex sola naturali Philosophia colligere licet non posse animum humanum vel minimam cogitationem subire quin velit Deus et ab aeterno voluerit ut subiret.' (*Ep.* I, viii, pp. 22–3.)

[2] *Princ.* I, 21 ; cf. *Med.* III, *l.c.*, and *Resp.* V, p. 369 : 14 f.–p. 370 : 12. For the intimacy of the connexion between Descartes' doctrine of time and his argument for the existence of God see the Appendix to *Resp.* II, where the discreteness of the parts of time is the axiomatic foundation of the *a posteriori* argument.

necessary or causal connexions between things, so the very word thing has lost its meaning. Qualities may conceivably be changed within the substance and substances themselves may conceivably interchange with one another.[1] To deny these possibilities is to deny the divine power ; that we cannot understand them is no argument, because the understanding of man is incompetent to fathom the nature and purposes of God. In so far, therefore, as science depends on the observation and discovery of regular sequences, Descartes' insistence on the omnipotence of God has led to the same intellectual chaos as we have noted before.

§ 5. *The Collapse of the Method and the Appeal to Revelation*

A similar chain of consequences may be traced out in Descartes' doctrine of man. When man draws near in order to investigate the facts of the universe his impotence is manifest from two sides. The world depends so intimately on God as to be beyond all ascertainable law and so beyond

[1] All these consequences, famous later under the name of Occasionalism, are drawn explicitly in the explanation of the Eucharist in the Reply to Obj. IV ; cf. e. g. ' nihil est incomprehensibile aut difficile in eo quod Deus creator omnium possit unam substantiam in aliam mutare . . . ' (p. 255 ; 9–11) ; ' . . . ex eo quod dixerim modos absque alia substantia cui insint non posse intelligi, non debet inferri me negasse illos absque ipsa per divinam potentiam poni posse, quia plane affirmo ac credo Deum multa posse efficere quae nos intelligere non possumus ' (p. 249 : 9–13). This explanation is constantly referred to by Descartes in his letters as being one of the attractive features of his philosophy, cf. e. g. *Ep.* I, cxiv, p. 367 : ' Dicam vero insuper me neutiquam metuere ne quid adversus fidem in illis occurret ; nam e contra ausim dicere illam rationibus humanis numquam ita suffultam fuisse, ac erit, si Principia mea admittantur ; maxime vero transubstantiatio quam Calvinistae arguunt, quasi ex vulgari Philosophia inexplicibilis esset, ex mea est facillima.'

Such statements are by no means hypocritical, as has sometimes been supposed, because the explanation given does, as a fact, spring out of the very heart of the system.

all investigation; but even if the world were of such a character as to be open to investigation, man is so imperfect that he could make little use of the opportunity. The feebleness of the powers of man in itself renders him incapable of approaching the works of God, to understand which indeed in their perfection and true limit would demand a divine revelation.[1]

This insistence on revelation is of course not illogical. Assuming the completely transcendent character of the infinite, it is only through revelation that knowledge can reach down to the finite. Indeed the illogicality is rather the other way. If the finite is so imperfect, the point to wonder at is that even through revelation it attains and grasps knowledge at all.[2] And so Descartes writes in language that, in view of his original starting-point, we can hardly understand: 'Thus if God reveals to us . . . certain things concerning Himself which surpass the range of our natural power of intelligence, . . . we shall have no difficulty in believing them, although we may not clearly understand them.'[3] But he goes still further. We must not only believe revealed truths although we do not clearly understand them; we must believe them although we clearly understand to the contrary. 'We ought to submit to divine authority', he writes, 'rather than to our own judgement, even though the light of reason may seem to us to suggest with the utmost clearness and evidence something else.'[4] In this one sentence is comprised the fundamental contradiction of his metaphysic. The doctrine of God as transcendent will is fundamental in his philosophy. Yet its implications annihilate the objects of the new logic. God is so perfect that it is only through revelation that we can have knowledge of the highest truths; but if truth is inaccessible,

[1] *Princ.* III. 1–2, and I. 24.

[2] 'Est *de natura infiniti* ut a nobis qui sumus finiti *non comprehendatur.*' (*Princ.* I. 19.)

[3] *Princ.* I. 25; cf. I. 28 (end).

[4] *Princ.* I. 76.

indeed opposed, to the natural reason, the need for a new logic, or for any logic at all, falls to the ground. The form in which Descartes accepted the doctrine of Divine Omnipotence is incompatible with his aspirations for the progress of human thought. The problem is, which to choose; and Descartes with no uncertain voice chooses the former. In order to save a theory about God he is ready to sacrifice his discovery of man.

The incapacity of man to cope with the problems presented to him by nature is increased when we consider the relatively subordinate part played in him by intellect. Although the basis of the Cartesian system is professedly the thinking self, it is not from thought but from will that it sets out. Will is prior to thought. Assent or dissent is the essence of the judgement; in the very act of doubting there is involved a refusal to believe, and refusal is the work of the will.[1] Compared with the work of the will in thought, that of the understanding is insignificant. The understanding is limited to what it has before it; it cannot pass beyond the immediately present clear idea. The will however is unlimited; it extends to and embraces everything in earth or heaven; and by thus asserting itself beyond the confines of the understanding drags us into the rash judgements of error.[2] Not only therefore is the will an essential element in thinking; it is the essential and the

[1] *Princ.* I. 6, 34, and 39; and *Ep.* I. xcix (=Notes against a Programme), p. 329: 'Quippe ego dixi, eas [=animae proprietates] omnes referri ad duas praecipuas quarum una est perceptio intellectus, alia vero determinatio voluntatis, quas noster [=Regius] vocat, intellectum et voluntatem; ac deinde illud quod vocavit intellectum dividit in perceptionem et iudicium; qua in re a me dissentit: ego enim cum viderem, praeter perceptionem quae praequiritur ut iudicemus, opus esse affirmatione vel negatione ad formam iudicii constituendam, nobisque saepe esse liberum ut cohibeamus assensionem etiamsi rem percipiamus, *ipsum actum iudicandi* qui non nisi in assensu, hoc est in affirmatione vel negatione consistit, *non retuli ad perceptionem intellectus sed ad determinationem voluntatis.*'

[2] *Princ.* I. 35; *Med.* IV; *Resp.* V, p. 377: ll. 8–16.

decisive element. It is not to be wondered at then that Descartes calls the will, rather than the understanding, the principal perfection of man.[1] Will is the primary fact about man as it is the primary fact about God.[2] The metaphysical motive of Cartesianism therefore is purely voluntaristic. Understanding in both man and God is overshadowed by the unlimited will.

The contradictions of the logic therefore are not solved but emphasized in the metaphysic. The isolation of the various individual products of intuition is paralleled by the isolation of the parts of time and the simple natures in the created universe, and these have their correlates in the isolated volitions and intellections of man. The system is essentially consistent and homogeneous. All finite things are isolated entities proceeding immediately from the direct action of the will of God. What is true of the created universe as a whole is true of the human mind, that is, if one has a right to speak of the 'human mind' at all. As Descartes wrote to a critic who had objected that the whole argument depended on what was meant by time: 'It is perfectly clear that no succession in our thoughts, like that in the divine thoughts, can be admitted. We understand clearly that it may happen that I exist in this moment in which I think a certain thought and yet that I should not exist in the immediately following moment in which I should be able to think another if it chanced that I should still exist.'[3] There are then no intrinsic connexions between things and no connexions between ideas, and no connexions in our thinking. For the pursuit of knowledge then there is one chance only left. If there is a real succession in the divine thoughts, then, we may say, knowledge is possible.

[1] *Princ.* I. 37.

[2] They are left irreconcilable (see e. g. *Princ.* I, 40, and *Eps.* I. viii–ix, to Elizabeth), for reasons which will become apparent in our discussion of the Cartesian substance (below, pp. 87–89).

[3] *Ep.* II, iv, p. 15.

The problem of the logic may be solved at the very last by the application to logic of the idea of God as a conserving cause, provided that, but provided only that, the conservation be conceived of as proceeding by some intelligible principle. If God may be shown to conserve in a way which we can understand, then, although all connexions, whether in our thinking or in the created universe, are external and are due to God alone, we may yet speak of a rational universe.

§ 6. *The Final Rally and the Eternal Verities*

The most striking form under which the problem was attacked by Descartes was that of the validity of the eternal verities. The eternal verities are the axioms of thought; and the problem is, whence do they derive their axiomatic character.[1] There are three possibilities. They may be independent of God; or dependent on Him in such a way that He cannot will their contrary; or dependent on Him absolutely. Of these three possibilities the two former would have preserved for man the hope of achieving knowledge, though the first at least would have been difficult to harmonize with the claims of conventional theology. But Descartes was uncompromising. He chose the third; and with this choice the logic crumbles to the ground.

The point is so important as to merit a closer scrutiny.

'When we apprehend that it is impossible that anything can be formed of nothing,' Descartes lays down in the first book of the *Principia*, 'the proposition "ex nihilo nihil fit" is not to be considered as an existing thing, or the mode of a thing, but as a certain eternal truth which has its seat in our mind and is a common notion or axiom. Of the same nature are the following: "It is impossible for the same thing to be and not to be at the same time"; "what has been cannot

[1] Cf. the eighth difficulty in the sixth set of *Objections*, pp. 417: 6–418: 9.

be undone"; and "he who thinks must exist while he thinks"; and so with very many other propositions the whole of which it would not be easy to enumerate. But we cannot fail to recognize them when the occasion presents itself for us to do so . . .'[1] The eternal verities therefore are those fundamental axioms of thought the truth of which is perceived intuitively by the mind and which though overlaid by subsequent prejudice may be considered to be the mind's native equipment in the work of thought. But these are not the only verities which are eternal. In the *Meditations* Descartes had spoken of 'an infinitude of particulars respecting numbers, figures, movements, and other such things whose truth is so manifest and so well accords with my nature that when I begin to discover them it seems to me that I learn nothing new or recollect what I formerly knew'. As an example he had given the case of the properties of a triangle, whose nature, form, or essence, he said, 'is immutable and eternal and in no wise depends on my mind'. From the point of view of the logic of the clear idea Descartes was right in making this affirmation, because the adoption of the criterion of clarity and distinctness involves the eternal validity of such truths as are clearly and distinctly perceived, and therefore of the truths of mathematics quite as much as of the idea of God. Gassendi, however, pointed out that the independent existence of these eternal, immutable essences and truths was incompatible with the omnipotence of God, since it would posit eternity and immutability apart from the will of God. Descartes in his reply turned the flank of the criticism by affirming that both in regard to their essence and existence, these eternal truths, including the truths of mathematics, are themselves dependent on the unconditioned will of God; God is not bound by them, nor are His actions or thoughts restricted by them. But in order to save their validity he goes on to say that they are in fact valid and eternal because God willed them so to be.[2] General-

[1] *Princ.* I. 49.

[2] *Resp.* V, p. 380: 1–13.

izing from this statement we come to the view of knowledge to which we were led as the only possible answer to the questions of the logic. In the problem of the eternal verities it comes out clearly. God is the conserving cause both of the axioms of thought and of the courses and norms of human investigation. He stands, as it were, as the 'everlasting arms' in which all things and all thoughts rest. 'To one who pays attention to God's immensity, it is clear that nothing at all can exist which does not depend on Him. This is true not only of everything that subsists, but of all order, of every law, and of every reason of truth and goodness.'[1] There is science, therefore, because, and only in so far as, there is a God.

Important passages from the letters confirm this presentation. Eternal verities, geometrical truths, essences of things, are all alike immediate productions of God as efficient and total cause. One cannot ask after the reason for any member of any one of these classes, any more than after that of any other. Just as God might have made the essence of a table different from what it is and just as He might or might not have created the world according to His inscrutable pleasure, so He might have willed that the radii of a circle should be unequal to one another; or that the three angles of a triangle should not have been equal to two right angles; or that contradictory statements should have been true at the same time. The eternal truths are not outside God and recognized by Him as such; they are eternal and true because recognized by Him. If God did not exist, they would not continue to be; just as they were created at His pleasure, so they depend for their continued existence upon the conservational activity of His will.[2]

From the point of view of logic, the problem clearly centres round our conception of the nature of the will of God; because

[1] *Resp.* VI, p. 435 : 22–6. See the whole paragraph to p. 436 : 25, and cf. p. 432 : 9–18.

[2] *Ep.* I, cx, p. 351 ; I, cxii, p. 359 ; I, cxv, p. 372 ; II, civ, p. 341.

our prospect of acquiring knowledge depends obviously on how far we can hope to understand, and, as it were, anticipate, the will of God. If we can understand the will of God, however imperfectly, knowledge may be held to be attainable. We may grant that it was the will of God that called all things and all thoughts and all the connexions between things and all the connexions between thoughts, into being, if only we can catch a glimpse of the working of that will. What, we may ask, is the relation of the will of God to the intellect of God, and what the relation between the intellect of God and the understanding of man ?

To the former question Descartes has been held to give an answer which, from the point of view of the building up of human knowledge, seems to be satisfactory. The intellect of God and the will of God are one ; God understands what He wills and wills what He understands, by one simple, indivisible action. The universe, therefore, is not, it would seem, a chaos, because the will of God is, as it were, intellectualized.

That this interpretation [1] gives precisely the opposite of Descartes' meaning is clear not only from a general consideration of his philosophy but from a stricter examination of contexts.[2] His aim was not to intellectualize the will of God, but to voluntarize His intellect. The intellect of God is one with His limitless will. The eternal truths do not radiate from God as rays from the sun,[3] so that from them we might be able to infer somewhat of the nature of God and the course of His will ;

[1] Cf. Saisset, *Essai de Philosophie Religieuse* (Paris, 1859), pp. 37–8.

[2] The stress of the passages is not on the fact that God's will works in accordance with the demands of intellect but that the activity of God is not complex as in the case of man but simple. 'Nullo modo Deum sentire putandum est sed tantummodo intelligere et velle ; neque hoc ipsum ut nos per operationes quodammodo distinctas, sed ita ut per unicam semperque eandam et simplicissimam actionem omnia simul intelligat, velit et operetur.' (*Princ.* I. 23.) This is brought out very clearly in Spinoza's account, where the unity of intellect and will in God is a corollary from His simplicity. (*Princ. Phil. Cart.* I. 17.)

[3] *Ep.* I, cx, p. 351.

but each individual one is a separate creation without any intelligible or necessary content in itself or connexion with any other. Even assuming then that the human intellect were by nature capable of the investigation of the universe (and we have seen that it is not), it would be met at every step by, as indeed in the final analysis it draws its own strength from, a power, which, as far as man is concerned, is completely non-rational; and which, for anything man can understand to the contrary, may be definitely irrational. Descartes presses this view so far as to say that the very logical necessity of the axioms of thought proves that they do not partake of the essence of God, because if they did, they would partake of His incomprehensibility as well.[1] The very presence then of what we call reason is a sign of the absence of the essence of God. By insisting on the transcendence of God, Descartes has over-reached himself. God, howbeit conceived as conserving cause, is so transcendent that His ways are unintelligible; and rational knowledge completely disappears.

§ 7. *The Resulting Scepticism*

The argument we have been discussing is, apart from its unfortunate close, only another example of the circular character of any argument in which the Cartesian God is concerned. We know nothing of God except through the aid of eternal verities, and it is therefore a glaring contradiction to treat them as dependent on His will. Descartes is brought back again and again to the original 'discrete' idea. All attempts to solve the original and primary difficulty of the

[1] '. . . quia mathematicas veritates perfecte comprehendunt non vero existentiam Dei, minime mirum est, si non credant illas ab hac pendere. Sed contra iudicare deberent quod, *quandoquidem Dei potentia intellectus humani terminos excedit, istarum autem veritatum necessitas cognitionem nostram non superat, sequatur illas esse minus quid et potentiae huic incomprehensibili subordinatas.*' (*Ep.* I, cxii, p. 359.)

logic have failed and we may now study it in its fullest consequences.

If thought cannot cohere with thought in the individual mind, then the individual mind cannot accord with other individual minds ; the unity which we deny to exist within the one, cannot spring up miraculously between the one and other ones. What appears to one man to be true may not be true for others, because, confined as the individual is within the bounds of his own ' clear and distinct ' idea, he can know and can pretend to know nothing about the ' clear and distinct ' ideas of others. Even within the individual's own mind the clear idea brings with it no compulsion, for of his free will he may refuse to give it assent ;[1] but if that be so within himself, how can he dream of its exercising compulsion both in himself and in another ? There is then no cogency in argument and no universal truth. The very idea of God is itself the fruit of a merely personal speculation. ' For my part ', writes Descartes to an anonymous correspondent, ' I would venture to say that I have found one proof which completely satisfies me and from which I know that God exists with more certainty than I know the truth of any proposition of geometry, but *I do not know whether I can make another understand it in the same way.*'[2] And this same note precisely is struck in his remarks to his intimate correspondent, almost

[1] ' Atque hic dicam me numquam negasse quin positiva haec facultas esset in voluntate. Contra enim existimo eam adesse non solum quoties voluntas determinat se ad istud genus actionum in quibus nullo rationis pondere in ullam potius quam in aliam partem inclinatur, sed etiam in omnibus eius aliis actionibus ; ita ut voluntas numquam se determinet, quin illam exerceat ; eousque ut etiam cum evidentissima aliqua ratio nos ad aliquid inclinat, licet moraliter loquendo vix possimus contrarium facere ; tamen absolute loquendo possimus ; *est enim semper nobis liberum, abstinere a prosequendo bono aliquo quod sit nobis clarissime notum aut ab admittenda veritate quapiam evidente* ; modo solum cogitemus bonum esse hoc ipso testari arbitrii nostri libertatem.' *Ep.* I, cxii (to Mersenne), p. 360 ; cf. above p. 30, n. 1.

[2] *Ep.* II, ciii, p. 334.

philosophical confessor, Mersenne: '. . . At least I consider that I have found an argument by which metaphysical truths may be demonstrated more evidently than any propositions of Geometry. I say this in accordance with my own opinion; for *I do not know whether I can convince others of it.*'[1] This repeated statement, it may be said, was made only 'in his haste', when he found that his demonstrations were not so generally accepted as he had expected. But in fact it is a direct consequent from the original premisses, and if Descartes had not made it expressly himself, we would have made it for him.[2] If to be true an idea must be discrete, then the communication of knowledge is as impossible as its discovery.

Conclusion: knowledge and the discrete idea. So the rationalism of Descartes results in a complete scepticism. 'Good sense or Reason' may be, as the opening paragraph of the Discourse affirms, 'by nature equal in all men'; but it is also particular and individual to each man. 'Diversity of opinion' does not proceed from some men being '*more* rational' than others, but by their being, if one may say so, *differently* rational from others. Descartes' very insistence on the fact of the individual possession of truths has led him to the

[1] *Ep.* II, civ, p. 340.

[2] A very similar criticism was made by Leibniz. 'Cartesii ratiocinatio de Entis perfectissimi existentia supposuit Ens perfectissimum intelligi posse, sive possibile esse. Hoc enim posito quod detur eiusmodi notio, statim sequitur existere illud Ens, quoniam ipsum tale finximus ut statim existentiam contineat. Quaeritur autem an sit in nostra potestate tale Ens fingere, sive an talis notio sit a parte rei, clareque ac distincte sine contradictione intelligi possit. Dicent enim adversarii talem notionem Entis perfectissimi sive Entis per essentiam existentis esse chimaeram. *Nec sufficit Cartesium provocare ad experientiam* et allegare quod idem eiusmodi in se clare distincteque sentiat, *hoc enim est abrumpere, non absolvere demonstrationem,* nisi ostendat modum per quem alii quoque ad eiusmodi experientiam venire possint; *quotiescumque enim inter demonstrandum experientias allegamus, debemus aliis quoque modum ostendere faciendi eandem experientiam . . .*' Stein, *Leibniz und Spinoza* (Berlin, 1890), p. 282. For the context see below, p. 78.

explicit denial of a universal truth. In so far then as he was in search of, and believed himself to have found, a logic which should help in the discovery of, and provide a theory for, truth, he must be pronounced to have failed.

The following chapter will attempt to demonstrate that this failure of Descartes was clearly and expressly recognized by Spinoza, and that it was precisely on the question of the possibility of the building up of a logic on the basis of discrete 'clear and distinct' ideas that the primary cleavage between the two thinkers arose.

II. SPINOZA

Introductory: The Form of the Ethics

BEFORE considering the systematic logic of Spinoza,[1] it will be convenient to deal with the problems presented by the actual form of his principal work, the *Ethics*.

As is well known, the suggestion of its peculiar method of presentation was derived from Descartes. At the end of the second set of objections, collected by Mersenne from various theologians and philosophers, there occurs the following passage: 'In order that it may be profitable for each and all to read your meditations, containing as they do so much subtlety, and, in our opinion, so much truth, . . . it would be well worth the doing if, hard upon your solution of the difficulties, you advanced as premisses certain definitions, postulates and axioms, and thence drew conclusions, conducting the whole proof by the geometrical method in the use of which you are so highly expert.'[2] This proposal to present non-geometrical matter in geometrical form was not novel,[3] as, indeed, is suggested by the fact that Descartes received it

[1] All references to Spinoza are from Bruder's edition; except for the letters, which are quoted by the numbering and pages of Van Vloten and Land's first edition (1883); and the Short Treatise, which is quoted by the pages and lines of Wolf's English version (A. and C. Black, 1910).

[2] *Obj.*, p. 128: 14–17.

[3] To the references of Dilthey (*Gesam. Schr.* ii, pp. 272–3, 278) and Freudenthal (*Leben*, p. 113) may be added the curious passage of Albert to which attention was directed by Jourdain (*Recherches*: Paris, 1843, pp. 445 f.): 'Accipiemus igitur ab antiquis, quaecumque bene dicta sunt ab ipsis, quae ante nos David Judaeus quidam ex dictis Aristot. Avicen. Algaze. et Alpharab. congregavit, *per modum theorematum ordinans ea, quorum commentum ipsemet adhibuit, sicut*

without surprise. He pointed out, however, that the analytic method of proof which he had employed in the *Meditations* is also essentially geometrical, and, as opposed to the synthetic method, which is the geometrical method as generally understood, has the great advantage of revealing to the reader the process by which the author himself came to his conclusions. It suffers, however, he says, from the defect that it only persuades a reader who is of like mind with the author, and who is open to be led gradually along the road of the discovery of truth. When, therefore, the reader is likely to be hostile, and only then, it is necessary to adopt the synthetic method of proof, because, in a close chain of propositions, each one depending on the preceding, misunderstandings and disagreements are easily tracked down and quickly removed.[1] To Descartes, therefore, the whole value of the synthetic method of exposition is just this rigid certainty of demonstration.

A consideration of the method as it appears in the work of Spinoza reveals precisely the opposite conception. It is first of all not a method of proof, but an order of presentation, as may be proved not only by the very title of the *Ethics*, but

et Euclides in geometris fecisse videtur: sicut enim Euclidis commento probatur theorema quodcunque ponitur ita et David commentum adhibuit, quod nihil aliud est nisi probatio theorematis propositi.' (*De Causis et Processu Unius*, II, tract. I, cap. 1.) [The Pseudo-Aristotelian 'De Causis', to which reference is supposed to be made, hardly answers to this description.]

It is interesting to note that Meyer, in the third paragraph of his introduction to the *Princ. Phil. Cart.* (p. 4), speaks of a few authors before Descartes who had tried 'ut *reliquas, ultra Mathesin, Philosophiae partes, methodo* atque certitudine *mathematica demonstratas* posteritati relinquerent'. He himself confesses to have made the attempt, before he knew of Spinoza's work, on the Cartesian philosophy (ib. § 5, p. 6).

[1] *Resp.* II, p. 155 foll. Cf. Joachim, *Study*, p. 10. 'Omnia ea quae in tractatu meo explicabam,' he writes to Mersenne (*Ep.* II, lxxvi, p. 249), 'a se mutuo ita pendebant, ut si scias illorum unum esse falsum, satis habeas ad concludendum rationes quibus utebar omnes corruere.'

also by the fact that Spinoza proposed to deal in precisely the same way with the intricacies of Hebrew Grammar.[1] In the *Ethics* itself the geometric form, even as an order, is dropped at convenience. The most characteristic portions of the work are to be found in the excursuses on particular problems in the appendices and longer scholia. In many passages he has stepped aside altogether and vindicated his method or results;[2] in many others he has gathered up the threads of a past argument, or sketched out the path for the future.[3] Now he gives a detailed criticism of current views;[4] now develops a particular point of special interest of his own.[5] And all in order to lead men, as he phrases it, 'by the hand', to the 'knowledge of the human mind and its highest beatitude'.[6] The geometric order could hardly have been regarded as the highway to truth by a man who by its help had calmly 'demonstrated' propositions which he expressly repudiated.[7]

It would, however, be unfair to Spinoza to affirm that the

[1] 'In animo semper habuit Hebraeam grammaticam, more geometrico demonstratam, luci exponere.' (*Pref. Op. Post.*, ap. Bruder, vol. iii, p. 275.)

[2] e. g. *Eth.* II, App. (the practical value of the system); III, pref. (the mathematical method in ethics); IV, 18 sch. (the essential piety of utilitarianism).

[3] e. g. III, App. (the passions); IV, App. (summary of ethical teaching); IV, 73 sch. (the free man's outlook); V. 20 sch. (power of mind in the control of emotion); V. 42 sch. (the freedom of the wise).

[4] e. g. I, App. (final causes and value judgements); V, pref. (Cartesian psychology); I, 15 sch. (infinity); I, 33 schs. (eternity and necessity); II, 48–9 schs. (will and intellect); V, 41 sch. (conceptions of immortality).

[5] e. g. IV, pref. (good and evil); II, 17 sch. (error); II, 40 schs. ('common notions'; grades of knowledge); III, 2 sch. (power of the body); IV, 17 sch. (ἀκρασία); IV, 35 sch. (asceticism); IV, 39 sch. (alternations of personality); V, 10 sch. (value of ethical maxims); V, 36 sch. (beatitude).

[6] II, pref.

[7] '. . . me non omnia quae in eo tractatu continentur, pro meis agnoscere, cum non pauca in eo scripserim quorum contraria prorsus

geometric order was one of convenience only, and nothing more. He adopted it for a definite reason, and that was its impersonality. Mathematics recognizes and has no place for personal prejudice. It neither laughs nor weeps at the objects of its study, because its aim is to understand them.[1] The great enemy to knowledge, Spinoza tells us, is man's habit of interpreting all things by the standard of his own likes and dislikes, and the consequent setting up of merely human norms by which the whole of Nature is judged. On the basis of this irrational prejudice men build up a superstitious theology, and, being too lazy and conceited to abandon it when they find it inadequate to meet the facts, erect finally their own ignorance into a god. 'It is easier for them,' he writes, 'to affirm the insoluble character of this and similar problems' (of teleology) 'and retain their present innate state of ignorance, than to pull down the whole construction and think out a new one. And so they hold it as a fixed principle that *the judgements of the gods surpass by far the grasp of the human mind*: a principle, forsooth, which in itself would have been sufficient to keep truth away from the human race for ever; had not mathematics, which deals not with ends, but only with the essences and properties of figures, pointed out to them another standard of truth.'[2] The mathematical method, therefore, meant to Spinoza the free unprejudiced inquiry of the human mind, uncramped by the veto of theology and theological philosophy. If we ask whose philosophy is here under criticism, the answer is clearly, the *philosophy of Descartes*. It was Descartes[3] who had laid it down *as a metaphysical canon* that 'the judgements

amplector . . .' (*Ep.* XIII, p. 46). Spinoza is annoyed with Blyenbergh for not having paid attention to Meyer's preface (*Ep.* XXI, pp. 94 and 98). He remarks on the irksome prolixity of the mathematical method in *Eth.* IV, 18 sch.

[1] *Eth.* III pref. For similar phrases cf. *Ep.* XXX, and *Tr. Pol.* I, § 4.

[2] *Eth.* I, app. pp. 217–18.

[3] See Meyer's pref., § 10 (p. 9), quoted below, p. 44; cf. *Eth.* I, 33, sch. 2. 'Verum neque etiam dubito si rem meditari vellent . . .

of God surpass the grasp of the human understanding', and so gave the sanction of the first philosopher of the age to the principle which would have been 'sufficient in itself to keep truth away from the human race for ever'. The mathematical method was held in esteem, then, by Spinoza, not because it was the method of Descartes, but because it was one [1] of the influences which helped to free him from Descartes. The form of the *Ethics*, in fact, far from being a tribute to Descartes, is the most vivid protest against his authority.

§ 1. *Spinoza and the Cartesian Logic: Meyer's Preface to the Principia Philosophiae Cartesianae*

That Spinoza was specifically dissatisfied with the logic of Descartes, and that he did not keep his dissatisfaction to himself, we have interesting and important contemporary evidence in the preface written to his account of Descartes' philosophy by his intimate friend Dr. L. Meyer. The oft-recurring statement that such and such a question surpasses the power of human comprehension, he says, must be remembered to be the opinion, not of Spinoza himself, but of Descartes. 'For our author considers that all those matters, and not those matters only, but also many others of greater sublimity and subtlety, can not only be clearly and distinctly perceived by us, but also are subject to the easiest of explanations, provided only that the human intellect is led to the investigation of truth and the knowledge of things by a *road other than that thrown open and laid down by Descartes*; and that therefore the principles of the sciences as laid down by Descartes, and everything built up by him upon them, do not suffice to unravel and resolve either all or the most difficult of the problems which meet us in meta-

quin tandem *talem libertatem qualem iam Deo tribuunt*, non tantum ut nugatoriam sed ut *magnum scientiae obstaculum* plane reiiciant.'

[1] '*Praeter mathesin* aliae etiam adsignari possunt causae a quibus fieri potuit . . . ut homines communia haec praeiudicia animadverterent et in veram rerum cognitionem ducerentur.' (*Eth.* I, app., p. 218.)

physics, but that *other principles must be sought for* if we wish to raise our intellect up to " that pinnacle of wisdom ".'[1]

The significance of this statement is only fully understood when we remember that it was made with the full knowledge and acquiescence, if not at the actual request, of Spinoza himself.[2] This preface is to be regarded as a manifesto of dissociation from Descartes. It is not only on the particular questions of metaphysical speculation that Spinoza is declared to be at variance with the man whose philosophy he is expounding, however weighty those questions may be ; but on the fundamental logical conceptions on which the whole structure of that philosophy was reared. And indeed, the two characteristic features of the Cartesian metaphysic which are specifically singled out as rejected by Spinoza[3] are just those which, in fact, confess the failure of the Cartesian logic. The God of Descartes was nothing more than an *asylum ignorantiae* ; while his doctrine of the impotence of human thought merely covered the impotence of his own method. Descartes had, in fact, sublimated his inability to meet the problems of metaphysics into the metaphysical principle of the incomprehensibility of phenomena.[4]

§ 2. *Central Problem : the Conception of God*

(*a*) *God as Asylum Ignorantiae.* Now Spinoza, like Descartes, affirmed the dependence of all things and thoughts on God,[5] but with an entirely different meaning. By Descartes,

[1] *Princ. Phil. Cart.*, pref., § 10, pp. 9–10. There seems to be in the concluding phrase a sarcastic reference to the letter prefixed to the *Principia* (quoted above, p. 15).

[2] See *Ep.* XIII. The parts of the preface to which he objected (*Ep.* XV) were evidently removed.

[3] Meyer's pref., §§ 9–10, pp. 8–9.

[4] ' Huius doctrinae sectatores . . . novum attulerunt modum argumentandi, *reducendo scilicet non ad impossibile sed ad ignorantiam, quod ostendit nullum aliud fuisse huic doctrinae argumentandi medium.*' (*Eth.* I, app., p. 219.)

[5] ' We know Him better even than we know ourselves, because

as we have seen, both thoughts and things are viewed as discrete entities, linked with their own pasts and futures, and with those of other entities, not by any inherent power of their own, or by any universal laws of connexion, but by the constant reinforcement of their being from the creative activity of God. Now the creative acts of God do not form a rational whole, that is, a whole such that, starting from any one constituent, we could infer the rest. And the reason is that the basis of inference is lacking. The course of the creative acts of God is determined by His ends, but His ends, though very real, are not intelligible to man. It is not to be doubted that such ends exist, or that the conception of ends in nature is valid; but, being the ends of a transcendent being, they are twice removed from the intellect of man.[1] We cannot, on the one hand, trace out connexions in things, because they do not exist; nor, on the other, can we understand the divine plan which causes such connexions to appear. The presence of a rational connexion in the universe, therefore, would be due to the accident that in this one case the divine will had coincided with the human understanding, but we have no guarantee that an accident which has occurred once will occur again. The discrete events remain discrete events. If we have a clear idea of any one, then we have a right to affirm its existence; but from this unique event no other can be deduced—at every step we must refer back to the immediate efficient cause of all, the working of which is beyond our comprehension. 'He had conceived the mind so distinct from the body,' runs Spinoza's criticism of the crucial difficulty of the Cartesian psychology and its characteristic resolution, '. . . that he was forced to take refuge with the cause of the whole universe, that is, with God.'[2]

without Him we could not know ourselves at all.' *Short Treatise*, II, 19 (p. 123); and often.

[1] *Princ.* I, 28; III, 2; *Med.* IV, p. 55: 23–6; *Resp.* V, p. 375: 7–9.

[2] *Eth.* V, pref. p. 390.

(*b*) *The modifications of the Principia Philosophiae Cartesianae in the Cogitata Metaphysica. God as Summa Intelligentia.* Traces of Spinoza's own opinion may be already found even in the *Cogitata Metaphysica*, a work which, with the *Principles of Descartes' Philosophy* to which it is appended, he by no means recognized as his own.[1] In it he takes over the Cartesian God, and, up to a point, and up to a point only, reveals his own position in its regard. Thus God is conceived of still as the conserving cause of the universe, but it is God as immutable and as infinite intellect.[2] God's existence and intellect and essence are one, and His power, too, is only one with His essence ; but this involves the position, not that God wills, and then understands what He has willed, but that He understands and, in the very act of understanding, creates.[3] It is, indeed, from this identification of the will with the understanding (not of the understanding with the will) that the immutability of God may be demonstrated ;[4] and so, too, His unity—because if there were many Gods the knowledge of

[1] In *Ep.* XIII he includes ' praecipua quae in metaphysicis tractantur ' with ' secundam partem Principiorum Cartesii ' as comprising the treatise which he had dictated to the pupil whom he did not wish to acquaint with his own opinions. It is not surprising, therefore, to find in it doctrines, e. g., as to the nature of time, which we know him to have definitely repudiated. But, although the *Cog. Met.* cannot be adduced as in any wise authoritative, it is legitimate to use it in illustration of discussions found elsewhere. Spinoza himself refers to some of its points later, e. g. *Ep.* XXI, pp. 91 and 92 ; *Ep.* LVIII, p. 210.

Freudenthal showed the strong influence of the Scholastic Revival in the *Cog. Met.*, but the edge of the argument, as M. Delbos has remarked (*Le Spinozisme*, Paris, 1916, p. 24), has been turned by the researches of M. Gilson, who, in his *Index Scholastico-Cartesien* (Paris, 1913), has demonstrated the close connexion between the Scholastics and Descartes himself.

[2] *Cog. Met.* II, 2 and 4.

[3] Ib. I, 2, § 3 ; II, 7, § 2 note, § 3.

[4] Ib. II, 4, note in Van Vloten's edition : ' Deum immutabilem esse clarius etiam apparebit, ubi eius voluntatem ab intellectu non differe, ostensum erit.'

each would be dependent on the others.[1] It is only as the object of His own knowledge that God may be said to create or to know created things; but since the knowledge of God is simple, it follows that His idea or decree concerning created nature is one.[2] Spinoza carries this stress on the conception of God as supreme intellect to its logical conclusion. Descartes had said that one must not be puzzled with the reflection that the will of man depends often on external things, and therefore might be conceived to be determined by them and not by God; because God is to be conceived of as having arranged these external things also according to His will. Spinoza transfers the suggestion from the sphere of will to that of intellect. It is true, he says, that God might have created things otherwise; but, seeing that man, too, is a part of created nature, he too would have been different in the universal change of all things, '*in order that he might be able to understand them*'. The remark is peculiarly significant in that it places the mind of man in the centre of things, and refuses to consider the very possibility of the universe being other than such as the mind of man could understand. But its significance is rendered even greater in view of the following sentence, in which Spinoza notes that by this one conception he has definitely broken with the philosophers who retained the traditional idea of God as transcendent will.[3] The emphasis is no longer on the power of God, but on the mind of man. And so he can say later: 'The philosopher does not inquire into what God can effect with His supreme power; but judges concerning the nature of things from the laws which God has implanted in them.'[4]

(*c*) *The new orientation; reason and necessity as opposed to will and freedom.* It is not difficult to disentangle the problems and solutions of the Cartesian and Spinozistic logics,

[1] *Cog. Met.* II, 2, § 2.

[2] Ib. II, 7, §§ 2–3, 6, 7 ('una tantum erit Dei idea sive decretum de Natura naturata').

[3] Ib. II, 9, § 3.

[4] Ib. II, 12, § 5.

however much they are involved in words and phrases which have long been emptied of their meaning. As we saw in the treatment of Descartes, the arguments touching the veracity and the concursus of God have a real logical significance. If we are to think at all, we must have confidence in the value and validity of thinking; and this confidence can spring only from the conviction of the existence of an intelligible order in that about which we are thinking. It is an irony that Descartes, who did so much to further the actual progress of the sciences, should, by reason of the premisses which he adopted, have been unable to find a logical justification for the very possibility of science. For the rational investigation of phenomena we need to be assured of two things, first, that we have the ability to reason, and, second, that the universe is such that we can reason about it. The first was denied by Descartes' subordination of intellect to will in man, the second by his affirmation of the incomprehensibility of the universe, which is only another aspect of the subordination of intellect to will in God. Both these positions must be rebutted if science is to be possible. As opposed, therefore, to Descartes, Spinoza held the identity of will and intellect in both man and God,[1] thus securing universal validity for the intellect of man; and by declaring God to be not the efficient and transeunt, but the immanent, cause of the universe,[2] secured its rationality by declaring its groundwork to be reason.

So far, then, it seems to us, Meyer's claim is justified. The foundation of Spinoza's logic is fundamentally different from that of Descartes, and it must therefore be regarded as a new

[1] e. g. *Eth.* I, 32–3; II, 48–9. *Tract. Pol.* II, § 6; *Ep.* XXI, p. 91 f.; LVI, p. 202 ('Si affirmamus Deum potuisse rem non velle' &c.); *Ep.* XIX, p. 67 ('Quia enim illa [Dei voluntas] ab eius intellectu non discrepat, impossibile aeque est, aliquid fieri contra eius voluntatem ac contra eius intellectum; hoc est, id quod contra eius voluntatem fieret, talis deberet esse naturae ut eius etiam intellectui repugnaret, ut quadratum rotundum').

[2] e. g. *Short Treatise,* I, 2, p. 30: 1–3; *Eth.* I, 18; *Ep.* LXXIII.

and distinct system. It is now clear why the controversy anent the freedom of the will assumed such importance in this crisis in the history of philosophy. It is not a psychological problem so much as a logical one. To Spinoza necessity is a *logical* theory. The universe must be such that it can yield its secrets to thought; thought must be capable of discovering those secrets. If either is unreliable, then there can be no science, and the pursuit of knowledge is a sham. The doctrine of necessity, therefore, stands at the very heart of Spinozism, as we have seen the doctrine of freedom to stand at the heart of Cartesianism. Just as the objections offered to Descartes centre around the problems attaching to the being and attributes of a creational Deity, and bring into question, not the doctrines themselves, but the method by which they were reached; so the objections offered to Spinoza scattered through the correspondence are directed for the most part against the idea of the scientific universe open to the investigation of the human mind. It makes no matter who it be—the secretary of the Royal Society in London, or the philosophizing merchant of Amsterdam, or the professor of metaphysics at Leyden, or the doctor of Utrecht, or the great Leibniz himself [1]—it is always the same charge again and again: here is a man who has dared assert that God, in the words of a modern writer,[2] 'must be conceived of as One who is absolutely faithful to His own methods, and who permits those methods to be scrutinized by man'. 'What!' cries the outraged Dr. Velthuysen, 'God cannot make a light weight lift up a heavier one, or a slow-moving body catch up one moving twice as fast!' and adds significantly, before passing the final judgement of 'atheism', this author 'refuses to go with Descartes, whose teaching, however, he would like to be

[1] *Ep.* III, V, LXXI, LXXIII–V (Oldenburg); XVIII–XXIV (Blyenbergh); XLII (Dr. Velthuysen); *Lebensgeschichte*, p. 228 (Professor Volder); and pp. 218 and 235 (Leibniz).

[2] Beard, *The Reformation* [2] (Hibbert Lectures, 1883), p. 392.

thought to have adopted, and affirm that just as the natures of all things are different from the nature and essence of God, so their ideas exist *freely* in the divine mind.' [1]

§ 3. *The Developed Doctrine*

(*a*) *The God of the Theology*. How Spinoza carried this conception of a rational Nature over into the realms of theology has been brilliantly expressed by an English expositor of the first part of the *Ethics*: 'He did not simply break off from theological speculation, and seek to establish philosophy on an independent footing; he seems intent on showing that theological speculation itself, when reason is once allowed free play, must at last purge itself of anthropomorphism and come round to the scientific view. Spinoza does not ignore theology, but provides an euthanasia for it; and there is every reason to believe that in so doing he faithfully reproduces the development of his system in his own mind . . .' [2] Whether Spinoza, in order to achieve scientific orientation, had any occasion or no to leave the theology from which he started, may be left for later consideration. It is, however, of supreme interest and importance to note that the characteristics which we have seen to be implicit in the Spinozistic God in the *Cogitata Metaphysica* are put forward without apology, and as self-understood, in the work which he devoted specifically to theology.

The third, fourth, and sixth chapters of the *Tractatus Theologico-Politicus*, which are nothing but a polemic against the Cartesians, illustrate this fact most clearly. They comprise the bold and clear affirmation of the reign of law, from the recognition of which, and of which alone, we can attain knowledge of God. If we break with the postulate of the rationality of Nature, then we break with the idea of God; from miracles we learn nothing but atheism.[3] To Spinoza, too,

[1] *Ep.* XLII, pp. 161 and 163.
[2] Pollock, *Spinoza* (ed. 1912), p. 155. [3] *Theol.-Pol.*, cap. 6, § 28.

as to Descartes, the arguments for the existence of God depend on the existence of the mind ; but it is not the mind as individual will, confined to the consciousness of its imperfection, but the mind as universal intellect, affirming and discovering itself in the very process of thought. From the one conception we are brought to the inference of the existence of an independent supreme will ; from the other to that of a self-dependent supreme reason. Or we may phrase the difference in another way. Descartes could only argue to the validity of thought from the existence of God ; Spinoza argued to the existence of God from the validity of thought. 'Since the existence of God', he says, 'is not known through itself, it must necessarily be inferred from notions the truth of which is so firm and unshaken that no power can be given or conceived by which they can be changed. To us at least from the time when we infer from them the existence of God, they must so appear, if we wish from them to infer it beyond all possibility of doubt. For if we were able to conceive that those very notions could be changed by any power whatsoever it might be, then we would be in doubt concerning their truth, and consequently even concerning our conclusion, i. e., the existence of God.' [1] The reference of the passage is clear. The Cartesian doubt can never bring to certainty ; and the Cartesian God, with His power to shake our belief in the validity of thought, is a self-contradiction.

It is to be noted that Spinoza is not satisfied with the mere conception of law as existing. Law must be conceived of, not only as existing in the abstract, but as knowable, that is to say, as open to the investigation of unprejudiced mind. The word 'miracle' may be understood in two senses, either as an actual break in the order of nature, or as an event which cannot be explained by natural causes. That belief in the former is the merest atheism we have already seen ; but belief in the latter is only a subtler and more dangerous form

[1] *Theol.-Pol.* VI, § 17.

of the same, for, implying as it does the doctrine that there are things which by their very nature are closed to the human mind, it puts a direct bar in the way of our only possible approach to truth and God. To speak of the transcendence of Nature and the incomprehensibility of the workings of God's will, far from saving the idea of God, destroys its meaning. Men only take sanctuary with the idea of God, he complains, when they cannot find a rational explanation ; whereas, as a matter of fact, it is only when they have a rational explanation that they may be said to be appreciating somewhat of the idea of God.[1]

(*b*) *The God of the Logic.* This parallel conception of the unity of God and the unity of created nature as a rational whole, which is the core of the *Cogitata Metaphysica* and the *Tractatus Theologico-Politicus*, is made the pivot of the specifically logical treatise, the *De Intellectus Emendatione.* That this early and unfinished treatise (which contains in brief space the essential doctrine of the Ethics) bears in its detail the mark of many extraneous influences, has been often pointed out.[2] For our purpose it is more important to note that as a whole it is specifically directed against any logical theory which sets out, as we have seen Descartes' logic to do, from the individual idea as discrete.

[1] 'Quia naturae potentia nulla est nisi ipsa Dei potentia, certum est, nos eâtenus Dei potentiam non intelligere quatenus causas naturales ignoramus ; adeoque *stulte ad* eandem *Dei potentiam recurritur quando* rei alicuius causam naturalem, hoc est, ipsam Dei potentiam, *ignoramus.*' (*Theol-Pol.* I, § 44.) '*Ex eo quod nostrum captum superat nihil intelligere possumus. . . .* Nos eo melius Deum Deique voluntatem cognoscere quo melius res naturales cognoscimus. . . . Ei igitur plane nugantur *qui ubi rem ignorant, ad Dei voluntatem recurrunt* ; ridiculus sane modus *ignorantiam* profitendi.' (Ib., cap vi, §§ 21, 22 23.) As the phraseology shows, the reference in every case is to the type of thought represented by Descartes.

[2] See Gebhardt's *Spinozas Abhandlung über die Verbesserung des Verstandes* (Heidelberg, 1905), and the same author's introduction to his translation in Meiner's series (Leipzig, 1907).

Taking without discussion the fundamental premiss that thought reflects reality, or, in Spinoza's terminology, that an idea contains 'objective' all that its 'ideatum', or correlate in things, contains 'realiter'; in order to understand the nature and significance of thought in general, we are told that we must study what a thought or idea is and involves. Since the thought or idea reflects a real thing, whatever is predicated of the thing is to be predicated of the thought. But in nature there are no things in the sense of discrete objects. Reality is a whole in which all things are inter-connected, and therefore to speak of a 'thing' is to use a false abstraction, there being in reality no separate things at all. Since, then, a thing has no existence apart from the system of things, it cannot be seized hold of by itself. As soon as we attempt to grasp it, it grows, as it were, under our hands, involving an ever-widening circle of connexions, until finally the process is only brought to an end by the bounds of the completed system itself. But what is true of things is true of ideas as well. Just in the same way, therefore, as a thing, so an idea, eludes our grasp, if we attempt to isolate it. An idea can be treated as discrete only if the thing it reflects is discrete, but a discrete thing, 'within the bounds of created nature', does not exist.[1] It follows that the very essence of an idea lies in its connexion with other ideas. There is, in fact, only one idea, i. e. the systematic unity of all ideas, as there is only one thing, the systematic unity of all things.[2]

This one idea is the norm of the mind's thinking with which the Spinozistic methodology begins, and the process of the mental development of the individual is just the process of approximation to it. But this conception is not to be taken in any mystic sense. No mere dreaming on 'absolute unity' is to bring the mind to perfection, and this for the reason that the 'objective' unity has a 'real' counterpart in

[1] *D. I. E.*, § 41.

[2] Ib., § 42; cf. § 76 with note 2.

the totality of Nature. The parallelism is so strict that as far as we are concerned the two are interchangeable. 'It is a self-evident truth that the mind understands itself more, the more it understands Nature.' From one point of view, the mind grasps the whole of Nature, only when it grasps or becomes the most perfect idea; from another, it only knows of, and approximates to, the most perfect idea, as it learns more and more of created Nature.[1]

It follows that there is a real order and a real progress in ideas. Theoretically speaking, the mind has only to be started on any one idea in order finally to arrive at the whole, since the idea involves precisely the same all-comprehensive system of connexions as is involved in the thing of which it is the idea. The 'concatenation' in either case is one and the same,[2] and it therefore makes no difference from which side the movement is begun. The criterion, then, of truth and of error, is precisely the length to which any suggested 'concatenation' may be traced. Error, like truth, quickly reveals itself as such, simply by the fact that, when followed out in its connexions, it does not, as does truth, result in and embrace the whole system.[3]

The process of human thought, therefore, and the process of created nature, are one and the same; the 'spiritual automaton'[4] and the universe which it sets out to investigate are constructed according to the same pattern. The human mind is simply a fragment of the totality of thought,[5] just in the same way as a thing is only a fragment of the totality of things, because the human mind is one with its ideas and its ideas reflect ideata from the world of things. The 'one true idea' of the logic and the 'God' of the theology are then one

[1] *D. I. E.*, §§ 39–40.

[2] 'Concatenatio intellectus . . . naturae concatenationem referre debet' (§ 95); 'anima . . . perget objective eosdem effectus formare' (§ 60 n.), and often.

[3] § 61; cf. § 104. [4] § 85. [5] § 73.

and the same ; and together they stand in a twofold relationship, on the one hand to their correlate, the totality of Nature, on the other hand to their part, the mind of man.

(*c*) *The God of the Metaphysic.* Leaving the various problems of the logic for later discussion, we may turn to the metaphysic in order to inquire into the nature of its fundamental premiss and its relation to the intellect of man. Spinoza's arguments for the existence of God are given in the eleventh proposition of the first book of the *Ethics.* After ten propositions have been allowed to pass without a mention of God, the demonstration is attempted that ' God or a substance consisting of infinite attributes, each one of which expresses eternal and infinite essence, necessarily exists '. This apparent paradox is due to the fact that Spinoza has taken over current philosophical terms, and by a close insistence on exact definition shown that they can only lead to his own views. The ' causa sui ' ; the ' substance ' ; the ' attributes ' ; the whole metaphysical terminology, in fact, which Descartes and the contemporary revivers of scholasticism had taken over from mediaeval thought ; all, when allowed to develop their own inner logic, result in the God of Spinoza. By the time he comes to the eleventh proposition, all he has to do is to substitute the word ' God ' for the word ' substance '.[1] The first demonstration, therefore, by the *reductio ad absurdum* method, is the only logical one : God is that the non-existence of which cannot be conceived.

This argument is only differently presented in the alternative demonstrations, which, in Spinoza's own words, all depend on the proposition that ' either nothing exists, or a

[1] It follows that the idea of God in Spinoza's system is prior to that of substance, as is shown by M. Delbos in a paper read before the Third International Congress at Heidelberg on ' La notion de substance et la notion de Dieu dans la philosophie de Spinoza ' ; cf. the same writer's *Le Spinozisme* (Paris, 1916), pp. 18–19 ; and below, p. 89.

being, absolutely infinite, necessarily exists as well'.[1] This fundamental conception of God as that which exists of itself, is not only the pivot of his whole philosophy, but also that which appears to have been considered in his own time as its characteristic and peculiar feature.[2] If we ask what it means to say that something 'exists of itself', and what significance it can possibly have for logic, we may refer to the first alternative demonstration. This turns again upon the point that the whole of things cannot be contingent, because a universal contingency is self-contradictory. We speak of the existence of any comprehensible object as possible, because we do not know whether the universe as a fact contains it, as we think it might. By the fact that it is comprehensible in thought we know that it has claims to be considered a candidate, as it were, for existence; but owing to our ignorance of the complete detail of the structure of things,[3] we cannot say positively whether it has or has not been admitted. Such a doubt applies to every thing except one, and that is clearly the whole structure of things itself. There can be no question of its failing to harmonize with its own self, and therefore of necessity it exists. The existence of God is involved in His own nature, but that is because there is nothing other than God. 'Whatever is, is in God, and nothing can be or be conceived without God.'[4] The two orders of the logic, therefore, the order of ideas and the order of things, are two expressions of one and the same unity,[5] which is *Deus sive Natura.*

[1] 'Ergo vel nihil existit vel ens absolute infinitum necessario etiam existit.' *Eth.* I, xi al., p. 194; cf. Joachim, *Study*, p. 45, and p. 51, n. 1 (on *Ep.* XII).

[2] *Epp.* XXXIV–VI. In *Ep.* XII Spinoza reminds Meyer that he had demonstrated it to him *viva voce* (p. 230).

[3] 'Res tantum ex parte novimus' &c., *Tr. Pol.* II, § 8; 'naturae ordinem . . . ignoramus . . .' ib. § 22, cf. *Theol-Pol.* IV, § 4, and XVI, § 11. The 'naturae ordo' is therefore a problem to be worked out and the way is left open to the purest empiricism. Cf. *Epp.* VIII–X (on definitions), and below, p. 96, with note.

[4] *Eth.* I, 15.

[5] *Eth.* II, 7 sch.

That this conception is historically not the end, but the beginning, of Spinoza's metaphysic, may be seen from an examination of the first chapters of his earliest work, the *Short Treatise concerning God, Man, and his Well-Being*. Here we find already fully expressed not only the opposition between contingent and necessary existents which leads us to the idea of the one, and only one, necessary existent, and the deduction of its immutability and perfection from the fact that outside it there is nothing; [1] but also its identification with the totality of nature from the very consideration of the unity of which its essential character may be deduced.[2] Our thesis that of itself it is sufficient to sever Spinoza's system once for all from that of Descartes may be finally illustrated from, and summed up in, a consideration of the first phrase and the key-word of the *Ethics*, the 'causa sui'.

(*d*) *God as Causa sui.* The question whether God may rightly be called 'causa sui' was raised by the priest Caterus in the first set of objections to Descartes' *Meditations*. The discussion centred round the conception of God as efficient cause, that is, in His characteristic function of creation, and Descartes finally affirmed that, since God preserves Himself in existence, He may be called the efficient cause of Himself or 'causa sui'.[3]

The interesting point to note is that Descartes views God consistently under the categories of will. Being and perfection are only other aspects of the power which enables any entity

[1] *Short Treatise*, I, 1, p. 18: 25 f.; p. 20: 19 f.; 2, p. 30: 2; II, 4, p. 45: 15 f.; 6, p. 49: 22 f.

[2] Ib. I, 2, p. 22: 3 f.; 24: 31 f.; 26: 34 f.

[3] 'Plane admitto aliquid esse posse in quo sit tanta et tam inexhausta potentia ut nullius unquam ope eguerit ut existeret neque etiam nunc egeat ut conservetur atque adeo sit quodammodo sui causa; Deumque talem esse intelligo.' (*Resp.* I, p. 109: 3–7.) Cf. the reply to Arnauld (p. 231: 24 f.): '... ubi tantum intellexi rationem propter quam Deus non indiget ulla causa efficiente ut existat, fundatam esse in re positiva, nempe in ipsamet Dei immensitate qua nihil magis positivum esse potest.'

to preserve itself. For this reason, as Descartes goes on to say, no human being may be said to exist *per se*, because he depends on an external power for his continued preservation.[1] Cause, therefore, to Descartes, means producing—and conserving—power, and, as Spinoza remarks, it is this conception of cause which underlies the very statement, '*Cogito, ergo sum*'.[2] Now, this efficient cause borrows its terminology from the vocabulary of effort. Its objects are graded as being, not more or less intelligible, but more or less easy of attainment. And so we see that the Cartesian axioms employed in the 'Arguments drawn up in geometrical fashion' in the appendix to the second set of objections, all of which turn upon the idea of cause, involve the terms 'easy' and 'difficult'. 'That which can effect what is greater or more difficult, can also accomplish what is less', is the eighth axiom; 'it is a greater thing to create or conserve substance than the attributes or properties of substance', is the ninth. On these two axioms the whole of the Cartesian *a posteriori* arguments for the existence of God are based, and their importance, therefore, cannot be over-estimated. But neither can their unintelligibility. 'For what does he mean by "easy"?' cries Spinoza in one of the few explicit criticisms of Descartes in his account of the Cartesian philosophy, 'and what does he mean by "difficult"? For nothing can be called difficult or easy absolutely, but only in respect of its cause; and so one and the same thing may be called both easy and difficult at the same time in respect of divers causes!'[3] Mere power or effort cannot be taken as a definition of essence. A thing 'is' not in so far as

[1] *Resp.* I, p. 111: 8–12.

[2] 'Si quis dubitare velit an ex nihilo aliquid fiat, simul poterit dubitare an nos quam diu cogitamus simus.' (*Princ. Phil. Cart.* I, 4, sch.)

[3] Ib. I, 7, sch. The note is characteristic: 'Ne alia exempla quaeras cape exemplum araneae quae telam facile texit quam homines non nisi difficillime texerent; homines contra quam plurima facillime faciunt quae forte angelis impossibilia sunt.'

it has power, but has power in so far as it ' is '.[1] We can only employ the idea of cause in the definition of God if we recognize that an efficient cause may be internal as well as external. But this is, of course, to destroy the notion of cause altogether, because such an immanent cause ' by no means produces anything outside itself.' [2]

The perfection, then, attributed throughout by Spinoza to God is not immensity of power, but self-completion of being. God, and the correlate of God, or Nature, ' is and is known through Himself '. He is ' the object of His own knowledge, or rather He is His own knowledge ', and to Him and His knowledge there is no such thing as a ' possibility ', but everything is actual.[3] In this logical sense He is a *causa sui*, a completely self-contained entity which cannot be thought away. So the very first words of the *Ethics* link up the whole movement of the various other expressions of Spinoza's philosophy, and throw into clear relief the nature of its primary and ultimate distinction from that of Descartes.

The clarity and distinctness of an idea, we may say, is indeed the test of its truth ; the fact of the human mind as thinking is indeed the foundation of knowledge ; God is the conserving cause of all, both of things and of thoughts, and of the connexions between things, and of the connexions between thoughts. But all this is because there is only one idea which, being self-explanatory, is clear, and only one idea which, there being nothing outside it, is distinct ; because the human mind thinks not in terms of now and here, and personal circumstances, but universally for all time, all places, and all

[1] *Princ. Phil. Cart.* I, 7, sch. second note (' vis qua substantia se conservat nihil est praeter eius essentiam ') with reference to the *Cog. Met.*

[2] *Short Treatise*, First Dialogue, p. 34 : 29 ; cf. ib. I, 3, p. 41 : 20 ; *Ep.* LX, p. 213 (' intelligo enim causam efficientem tam internam quam externam ').

[3] *Short Treatise*, Appendix I, prop. 4, proof and cor. (pp. 155–6) ; *Cog. Met.* II, 7 ; cf. the criticism of the idea of perfection in *Eth.* IV, pref.

men ; because the universal order of thought and the universal order of things are one in the self-subsistent system of the whole, which is God. The eternal verities are eternal and true ; God willed them so to be ; but ' willed ' them not in the sense of producing them as a casual and inconsequent creation. His will and intelligence are one with His essence, and therefore they flow from His free necessity as do properties from a mathematical figure. Without God, the *causa sui*, nothing can be or be conceived, not because God is absolute power, but because God is absolute reason.

III. MAIMONIDES

Introductory: The Ethics, The Tractatus Theologico-Politicus, and The Guide for the Perplexed

A CASUAL reader of Spinoza's philosophical works, seeing the homogeneity of their general outlook, would have, it may be imagined, a difficult task to arrange them according to the order of their composition. Logic, theology, and metaphysics, even the rough preliminary sketch of the system, present precisely the same fundamental characteristics; while the crowning work of the whole is artistically so perfect as to give the impression of being the product of one uninterrupted effort of thought. It is only when we turn to the letters that we gain any idea of the political and scientific interests that made Spinoza's philosophy something more than an abstract speculation; or of the human incidents of the life which appeared even to the contemporary observer to be confined within the tomb of a library.[1] The details of the general inquiry are beyond our scope; we must turn our attention however to one puzzling point.

When we find that in 1663 de Vries and his circle send questions to Spinoza relating to the *Ethics*; when in the letter to Blyenbergh dated 1665 reference is made to a treatment of 'cupiditas' in 'our *Ethics* yet unpublished', and, later in the same year, in a letter to an anonymous correspondent, to the 'third part of our philosophy' which evidently is none other than the fourth book of the *Ethics* which we now possess;[2] it is difficult to understand how it comes about that the complete work was not ready for publication before ten more years

[1] 'Sibi soli vivere videbatur, semper solitarius et quasi in museo suo sepultus.' The phrase is quoted by Kuno Fischer (*Spinoza* [5], p. 189).
[2] *Epp.* VIII–X; *Ep.* XXIII (p. 107); *Ep.* XXVIII (p. 121).

had elapsed. The explanation of this singular delay has been presented convincingly by Freudenthal.[1] The composition of the *Ethics* was deliberately interrupted in favour of what Spinoza considered to be the more immediately pressing treatise on freedom—the *Tractatus Theologico-Politicus.* That the *Ethics* and the *Treatise* should present such striking affinities is then not surprising. They spring from the same period of the author's life and are from the chronological point of view intimately intertwined. This fact has been generally acknowledged, but its significance for the investigation of the sources of Spinoza seems to have escaped notice.

Most students have remarked the erudition of the *Treatise*, an erudition which on the face of it was not acquired in a day. But it is forgotten that this profound learning, even if acquired originally in early youth, must have been recalled to memory during the period when the major portion of the *Ethics* was being composed. Nor could the results of this revisional study have been obliterated on the day of the appearance of the *Treatise* at 'Hamburg' in 1670. They must have remained during the years immediately following, the years, that is to say, during which the *Ethics* was revised and put into its final form. But this means that the *Treatise* is the key to Spinoza's philosophy and particularly to its matured expression in the *Ethics.* The thought of the *Ethics* is in the *Treatise*; that we have already seen. But the literary background too of the *Ethics* can be none other than that of the *Treatise.* Whatever source or material be sought for the *Ethics*, it must at least include the source and material of the *Treatise.* If then we can discover the material out of which the *Treatise* was constructed, we can say definitely and dogmatically that this material at least (whatever else may be suggested) was present to Spinoza's mind during the period of the composition of the *Ethics.*

[1] *Leben*, cap. 7, particularly 150–1, and 169–71; cf. Wolf, *Introduction to Short Treatise*, p. 74 f.

The importance of the point only becomes clear when we realize the literary difference between the two works. Both alike are dogmatic presentations of results, but whereas the *Ethics* only very occasionally indeed refers to other thinkers, the *Treatise* contains specific mention of, and even detailed abstracts from, books and opinions criticized or approved. In directing attention to these then we stand on no uncertain ground. It is not a question of possibility but of certainty. It is not difficult to show that similar ideas have occurred to the minds of more than one thinker, or that a phrase has been used in common by all the sharers in one cultural tradition. But when we are assured that it is certain that Spinoza made actual use of the work of Bruno,[1] for example, or of Telesio,[2] we must remember that, since there is not the slightest positive indication in support of the suggestion, we have no right to consider it, even if admitted at all, as anything more than a doubtful, although interesting, possibility. Even the evidence of the library list discovered towards the end of the last century cannot be considered conclusive in any direction. On the one hand we have grounds for thinking that Spinoza gave away the more rare and valuable of his books before he died ;[3]

[1] Subsequent writers seem to have added little to the material collected originally by Jacobi, although they have in almost every case neglected his caution. 'Mein Hauptzweck bei diesem Auszuge', he writes (Preface to the second edition of the *Spinoza-Briefe*, reprinted in Scholz' *Hauptschriften zum Pantheismusstreit zwischen Jacobi und Mendelsohn*, Berlin, 1916, p. 50) 'ist durch die Zusammenstellung des Bruno mit dem Spinoza, gleichsam die *Summa der Philosophie des "En kai Pan"* in meinem Buch darzulegen. . . . Schwerlich kann man einen reineren und schöneren Umriss des *Pantheismus im weitesten Verstande* geben, als ihn Bruno zog. Dass man aber diese Lehre . . . kennen lerne, um sie überall *wieder zu erkennen* . . . dieses halte ich . . . für ungemein nützlich . . .' [Original italics.] He was interested in Bruno, that is, not as a 'source' of Spinoza but as the type of pantheist.

[2] Dilthey, *Ges. Schrift.*, vol. II, p. 289 f.

[3] 'Inter Spinosiana praeter manuscripta praelo commissa nihil rari fuisse scias, nam ego ante et post eius obitum (tibi in aurem !) cuncta singulatim sim perscrutatus et quaecumque eruditionem aut

and on the other the presence of a book in a library is no proof of its having been read by, or of its having exercised any influence on, its possessor. But when a book is published bearing definite quotations from definitely named authors, one must suppose that these authors were read, and in some measure assimilated, by the writer. The *Tractatus Theologico-Politicus* therefore stands in relation to the *Ethics* from the point of view of the investigation of the literary sources of the latter in much the same way as do Locke's quotations from the contemporary literature of travel to the anthropological portions of the *Essay on Human Understanding* and the *Treatises on Government*—namely, as definite proof that in the period of composition the author's mind was exercised by certain definite books in certain definite directions.

This then is the ground of and apology for the following study of Maimonides.[1] The researches of Joel have shown conclusively that the whole of the earlier part of the *Treatise*, those chapters in particular dealing with prophecy and miracles,

raritatem redolebant amicorum et eiusmet (dum adhuc viveret) iussu transsumpsi . . .' (Letter of Schuller to Leibniz, November 1677, quoted in the appendix to Stein, *Leibniz und Spinoza*, p. 289.)

[1] Maimonides (=Moses ben Maimon, Maimûni, or Rabbi Moyses Aegyptius), born in Cordova 1135, died in Egypt 1204. For a general account of his life, works, and influence see: Abrahams and Yellin, *Maimonides* (Macmillan, 1903); L. G. Lévy's volume in the *Grands Philosophes* series (Alcan, 1911); and the collection of studies *Moses ben Maimon* (Fock, Leipzig, 1908 and 1914). The Guide was written originally in Arabic but was translated immediately into Hebrew and Latin (Spinoza's copy was the Venice edition of Ibn Tibbon's Hebrew), and it was in these versions that it exerted the very considerable influence on mediaeval and modern thought which is described by Kauffmann in an essay in *Stein's Archiv* for 1898, pp. 333–73 (reprinted in his *Ges. Schrift.*, Frankfurt, 1910, vol. ii, pp. 152–89), and by Guttman in the first volume of *Moses ben Maimon*. Modern students will use the great French version of Munk (*Guide des Égarés*, Paris, 1856–66) or the English of Friedlander. It is from the one-volume edition of the latter (Routledge, second edition, third impression, 1919), as being the most generally accessible, that all quotations have been made.

are so deeply impregnated, both implicitly and explicitly, with the teaching of the *Guide for the Perplexed* of Maimonides that without it they could never have been written.[1] Now precisely these chapters were ready, and their content known abroad by September 1665,[2] almost exactly the time when the 'third part of our philosophy' was being completed. Leaving aside therefore all other sources, certain or probable or possible, and neglecting any hypothetical reconstruction of studies which have left no explicit trace, we may take it as undeniable that for the period of time at least [3] between the commencing and final revision of the *Ethics*, the *Guide for the Perplexed* formed a highly important element in the background of Spinoza's thought. Our problem then is: What would Spinoza have learned from it, and what light was it likely to have thrown on the problems immediately before him?

§ 1. *The 'Guide for the Perplexed': General Characterization*

The 'perplexed' for whom Maimonides wrote the *Guide* are those men who, though desirous of retaining traditional belief,

[1] *Spinozas Theologisch-Politischer Traktat*, Breslau, 1870, e. g. pp. 9–10, and 59. Even Kuno Fischer in his attack on Joel's general theory admits that so far as the Biblical and exegetical inquiries of the Tractate are concerned, Joel was in the right (*Spinoza* [5], p. 266), an admission which, from our point of view, is sufficient. I may be allowed to add that, although in the following pages I have attacked the problem from a different angle altogether, it seems to me that the admirable pioneer work of Dr. Joel has been insufficiently appreciated.

[2] 'Video te non tam philosophari quam, si ita loqui fas est, theologizare; de *Angelis quippe, prophetia, miraculis*, cogitata tua consignas.' (Ep. XXIX, from Oldenburg, September 1665). Such opinions go back to Spinoza's youth and were the beginnings of the troubles which led up to his excommunication, if one may believe Lucas (cf. his *Life of Spinoza*, ap. *Lebensgeschichte*, p. 5).

[3] Spinoza's acquaintance with Maimonides goes back of course much earlier. See the evidence below, pp. 103–4.

are yet puzzled by the apparently contrary teaching of scie
and philosophy.[1] The *Guide* is the type (as it was in fact
model) of the scholastic contribution to thought, which, stripped of accidents of time and place, is the endeavour to effect a reconciliation between philosophy and religion, the science of rational thought and the art of revealed belief. Now in order to achieve this purpose two methods are possible. The apologist may either develop a purely rational system in philosophy and then proceed to demonstrate that there is nothing in religion incompatible with this system ; or he may first concede all the demands of religion, and then, finding that the result is at variance with the accepted claims of philosophy, devote his energies to the task of undermining these latter. These two methods of defending and preserving religious belief are common in the history of the world's thought. A notable example of the former is the rationalized Christianity of the Hegelians ; of the latter, the arguments for belief, based, in the phrase of a modern thinker, on ' philosophic doubt ', of which a pragmatic age is seeing a strong revival. Maimonides adopts the former alternative. Unwilling to abandon either religion or philosophy, he asserts their essential identity. Philosophy is true and religion is true, but since truth is one they are one in the one truth. To him then there is strictly speaking no such thing as theology at all. There is no need for a mediating science between philosophy and religion because there are not two contraries to be mediated.

In the *Guide*, however, we are presented with something other and more important than a series of positive propositions. A rational guide must point out not only what is the right road, but also what is the wrong ; and why and by what signs we are to recognize them and give the one preference over the other. And so we are given an account not only of the philosophical system of Maimonides but also of the pseudo-philosophical system against which it was directed. The

[1] Introduction, p. 2.

whole structure of the *Guide* is penetrated by a triplicity.[1] The opinion of the ordinary man as systematized by the theologian is set against that of the philosopher; and the opinion of the philosopher is itself subjected to a close scrutiny before it is modified and adopted or rejected. The result is that we have a complete presentation of the two antithetical points of view, the metaphysics of the theologian on the one hand and the theology of the metaphysician on the other. The theologian, in order to defend traditional belief, was driven to adopt a definite set of metaphysical premisses, premisses of so outrageous a character as to cause the student to fall into 'perplexity' as to whether he should abandon logic or religion. The *Guide* undertakes to show that the opposition is apparent only; that for the upholder of religion there is no need to reject the claims of thought or the results of science; that, indeed, without these latter, religion cannot stand. It is clear then that its principal quarrel is with the theologian. The main thesis of the present essay is that *in his defence of traditional belief the Arabic theologian was led to construct a metaphysical system which in logical essentials is precisely the same as that adopted long after by Descartes;* while that *in his attack on and rejection of this system Maimonides urged the same objections and put forward the same positive grounds of reconstruction as were used against Descartes by Spinoza.*

In the following discussion I propose to present the argument of the *Guide* as it would have appeared to Spinoza, that is, as a datum, not as a problem; and, neglecting all questions merely of historical or philological interest, to endeavour to seize its main metaphysical issues. It must be remembered that these are set forth, with a simplicity approaching baldness, in a volume which, even in the diffuse English version, comprises less than four hundred pages.

[1] Cf. Munk, vol. ii, p. 259, n. 2; and below, p. 129.

§ 2. *The Groundwork: Authority and Reason*

The first problem attacked by the *Guide* is that of authority. The great source of error and confusion in religious thought, we are told, lies in the literal interpretation of Biblical texts.[1] It is from them, as wrongly and uncritically understood, that the premisses are derived which the ordinary man considers himself bound to accept, but these premisses often run so counter to our intellectual convictions that their substantiation by the theologian necessarily involves a perversion of logic. From the very beginning then theology is crippled. Once accept without discrimination the authority of a body of text, and the theological method follows of necessity.

The theologian, considering it his duty to defend, for example, the anthropomorphic conception of God which is to be found in certain Biblical sentences, can only do so by manufacturing such principles with regard to the world and man that working back from them he may be able to arrive again at the particular conception of God with which he started, and so pointing to these principles be able to claim triumphantly the support of reason for his belief. Certain assumed qualities of the Godhead therefore are his starting-point, and on them he constructs his science of nature and of man. His physics is made to depend on his theology, because if God is of a certain nature it is clear that the universe cannot be such as to contradict it.[2] His anthropology is determined by the same *a priori* considerations. God allows us to know only

[1] Introduction, pp. 2 and 5; and e. g. I, 53 (p. 72).

[2] 'The earlier theologians when they laid down their propositions did not investigate the real properties of things; first of all they considered what must be the properties of the things which should yield proof for or against a certain creed; and when this was found they asserted that the thing must be endowed with those properties; then they employed the same assertion as a proof for the identical arguments which had led to the assertion and by which they either supported or refuted a certain opinion.' (I, 71, p. 109.) Cf. I, 75 end (p. 141); III, 15 (p. 279); and often.

so much as He wills. There is no science of logic, only the accident of revelation, a revelation which is open—or closed—to all alike.

In sharp opposition to the attitude of the theologian stands that of the scientist and philosopher—to Maimonides the two are indistinguishable. In his opinion the apprecia-tion of the universe and its problems is not a heaven-sent gift but the painful acquisition of long study. Not only then is the instrument of education mathematics, mathematics being the type of method and methodical research, but the very progress of education resembles that of mathematics in that it gradually passes from the apprehension of the more easy to that of the more difficult, in a slowly ascending scale.[1] From this consideration two most important consequences follow. The first is that all men are not equally capable of learning ; the second that not all things are equally susceptible to investigation. On the one hand therefore, in order to arrive at the highest truths the progress through the lower must be made ; on the other, it does not follow that, because the road is open, therefore every one is equally fit to take it.

It would seem then that the majority of mankind are con-demned for ever to ignorance. And so indeed they would be, Maimonides agrees, if a method had not been found by which they could be led easily to the results achieved by more powerful thinkers. This method was the expression of the highest intellectual truths in images to strike the imagination and so produce a vivid (if imperfect) impression on minds incapable of grasping the non-sensuous. This and this only is the aim of the Scriptures, which are nothing more than a means of bringing home, in as forcible a way as possible to

[1] 'Incipiendum a logicis, deinde tentendum ad mathematica ; inde versari oportet in naturalibus ; ultimo in divinis.' (Leibniz' note to I, 34.) The penetrating summaries and criticisms (on the Latin version of the *Guide*) made by this great thinker were discovered and edited by Count Foucher de Careil (*Leibniz, la philosophie juive et la Cabale*, Paris, 1861).

non-philosophical minds, the philosophical truth of the existence of a God.[1] It follows that they are by no means data to which the philosophizing mind must accommodate itself, but rather material to be accommodated to the demands of the philosophizing mind. If in the lapse of time the symbol has been taken for the essence, the image for the thought, the metaphor for the actuality; it becomes precisely the task of the thinker not to accept the mere shell, and that at its face value, as the theologian does, but to scrape away the incrustations of superstition and ignorance, and bring to the light again the truth concealed within.

Freedom of Thought. (*a*) *Maimonides.* The opening chapters of the *Guide* therefore, dealing with the anthropomorphic phrases of the Bible, strike the keynote of the whole. Whether from the historical or philological point of view the primary assumption is sound and the allegorical principle of textual interpretation legitimate, is a question on which varying opinions have been held.[2] Its interest for us however is not the fact but the logical motive. As against the theologian who started with this written authority and proposed to make his thought subservient to it, Maimonides asserts the principle of the primacy of thought and of the duty of the thinker to interpret authority. But if it is once laid down to be the duty of thought to interpret authority, then authority in the sense of external constraint disappears. The ultimate standard is the human mind, the deductions of which indeed are held to be so universal that the possibility that even texts derived from the remote past should be in opposition to them, cannot

[1] I, cap. 46, pp. 59 and 61.

[2] 'Que serait devenue l'humanité', remarks Renan in a brilliant passage (*Averroës*[3], p. 433), 'si, depuis dix-huit siècles, elle avait entendu la Bible avec les lexiques de Gesenius ou de Bretschneider? On ne crée rien avec un texte que l'on comprend trop exactement. L'interprétation vraiment féconde [est ce] qui, dans l'autorité acceptée une fois pour toutes, sait trouver une réponse aux exigences sans cesse renaissantes de la nature humaine . . .'

be entertained. To see a present truth in an ancient text is to free truth of the bounds of space and time. Far from being an anti-rational procedure it is the very apotheosis of the claims of reason; by denying it history it asserts its eternity. To the working out of this principle in detail the first half of the first of the three books of the *Guide* is devoted, and countless references throughout the whole work substantiate and drive it home.[1]

(*b*) *Spinoza*. Did Spinoza learn the lesson ? No reader of the *Theologico-Political Treatise* can doubt it. Indeed its professed aim is to demand the supremacy of reason in public and private life as the primary condition of civic security.[2] That the allegorical method had lost its force in Spinoza's eyes means not that he had abandoned, but that he had come to a fuller realization of, its rationalistic motive. The Maimonidean attempt to show the essential identity of philosophy and religion could not be held in the Europe of the seventeenth century, even in the 'free-thinking' Netherlands. It was necessary therefore either to join the other camp and 'accommodate metaphysics to religion', or else to seek some other hypothesis of their relation which would enable him, while bending the knee to religion, to 'think what he liked and to say what he thought'. How Spinoza regarded the former alternative we know from our earlier discussion of the *Theologico-Political Treatise*. There remained then the latter, to divide the spheres of influence of the two. The end of religion is affirmed to be not the attainment of truth but the inculcation of obedience. Since then it ceases to be the very core of intellectual life, as it was to Maimonides, the Maimonidean rationalism may be not only retained but reinforced. The

[1] A notable instance is severely censured by Spinoza (*Theol.-Pol.*, cap. 7, §§ 75–87).

[2] The title-page reads : 'Tractatus Theologico-Politicus, continens dissertationes aliquot, quibus ostenditur, libertatem philosophandi non tantum salva pietate et reipublicae pace posse concedi, sed *eandem, nisi cum pace reipublicae ipsaque pietate, tolli non posse*.'

need of the resolution of apparent discrepancies between philosophy and religion has disappeared, and thought is left supreme to work out its own uninterrupted salvation.

The crucial chapter of the *Treatise*, the fifteenth, to which all the earlier chapters are preliminary and all the later commentary,[1] is perfectly precise on the point and in the most marked way retains Maimonides' polemic against the anti-rationalism of the theologians while itself ostensibly a polemic against Maimonides' rationalism. 'Those who do not know how to separate philosophy from theology', he writes, 'dispute whether Scripture should be the handmaid of reason, or whether reason should be the handmaid of Scripture; that is to say, whether the sense of the Scripture should be accommodated to reason, or whether reason should be accommodated to Scripture. The former position is defended by the sceptics, who deny the certitude of reason; the latter by the dogmatists. Both sides are completely in error . . . To follow either involves the corrupting of either reason or Scripture. For we have shown that Scripture does not teach philosophy but only obedience and that everything contained therein is accommodated to the understanding and preconceived opinions of the vulgar. Whoever then wishes to accommodate Scripture to philosophy is sure to ascribe to the prophets many things which they had never thought of even in their dreams . . . while whoever makes reason and philosophy ancillary to theology is forced to admit ancient popular prejudices as divine . . .' The antithesis here is clearly presented. On the one hand theology and philosophical scepticism; on the other philosophy and textual rationalism. To Spinoza the latter combination failed only because it did not seem to him to go far enough. The 'certitude of reason' could not be

[1] '*Hoc usque*, Philosophiam a Theologia separare curavimus et libertatem philosophandi ostendere quam haec unicuique concedit. Quare *tempus est, ut inquiramus quo usque* haec libertas . . . se extendat.' (*Theol.-Pol.*, XVI, § 1.)

bound down by the 'dead words';[1] he did—or would—not see that the whole point of the method of allegorical interpretation was that the words were not dead. But whether or no Spinoza agreed with Maimonides in putting his own thought into the Scriptures, thought is declared to be supreme and autonomous[2] and the Maimonidean battle is won. Nor is the connexion concealed. The whole chapter is one long discussion of the views of 'the first . . . who openly pronounced that Scripture must be accommodated to reason—Maimonides.'[3]

§ 3. *The Theological Problem: The Attributes of God*

Having laid the foundation in the opening chapters of the *Guide*, Maimonides proceeds to the first of the great problems which he proposes to treat, the problem of the attributes of God. None of the great problems of a theological metaphysic seem to us so far away, yet none attack an inquiry with more vital consequences for the whole of general philosophy. If the process of knowledge is as a fact the finding of unity in diversity, then the answer to the problems of knowledge must be sought for in the nature of that unity and its relation to the diversity. In the practical investigations of the physical sciences the fact may be assumed; in the dialectic of the logicians, as easily concealed. It is only within the confines of a rigid and uncompromising theological monotheism that subterfuge is impossible. The supreme unity cannot suffer diversity; but the diversity, to all appearance, is more real than the unity itself. The long discussion of the attribute

[1] Ib. XV, § 10.

[2] Ib., § 42. There is a curious passage in a letter to Blyenbergh (*Ep.* XXI) in which the relations of truth and the Scriptures are discussed in a thoroughly Maimonidean spirit. 'Omnino in eo quod mihi intellectus monstrat,' he writes, 'acquiesco sine ulla suspicione, me ea in re deceptum esse, nec Sacram Scripturam, quamvis eam non investigem, ei contradicere posse; quia *veritas veritati non repugnat* . . .'

[3] Ib., § 4.

problem therefore is the essential preliminary to the positive exposition. If we follow out the course of the argument with a little patience and sympathy we shall see how far-reaching are the issues involved.

There are broadly speaking, Maimonides tells us,[1] two types of attributes ascribed by the theologians to God. The one expresses His nature extrinsically in terms of His creative activities, the other intrinsically in terms of His essential perfections.

The first type is connected with a particular view of the created universe. The created universe is the product, and continually presents new examples, of what appear to be different activities of God. Now the theory is that each activity is distinct and presupposes the workings of yet another aspect of God—just as it is believed, for example, that different human activities spring from different 'faculties' in the individual mind. For each single act of God therefore another attribute is sought, and there would logically be just as many attributes as there are activities, and as many activities as there are things.

This is the cruder type and is easily disposed of by pointing out the invalidity of the argument from diversity of product to diversity of cause. It is one and the same fire which bleaches and blackens, hardens and melts; one and the same mind which learns divers sciences and arts. We must either accept this possibility with regard to the divine attributes or acquiesce in an undisguised polytheism. What has really happened is that the diversity of created things has been set into the Godhead itself, and the unity of God been sacrificed to the variety of His creatures; but, as we shall see, the unity of God cannot be so lightly let go, because it is not only a verbal dogma but an intellectual necessity.

[1] I, cap. 53. The theory of attributes is given in I, caps. 50–60, and is thoroughly discussed by Kaufmann, *Geschichte der Attributenlehre* (Gotha, 1877), pp. 363–470.

The second type of attributes, the intrinsic, is no more tenable than the first, though for a far different reason. Just as we cannot transfer our conceptions of transeunt causality to God, so we cannot ascribe to Him our conceptions of perfection. Since God is not man, human perfections have as little place in Him as human imperfections; and it would be as absurd to speak of Him in terms of human virtues as to speak of Him in terms of human vices. And so we come to the result that we cannot speak of Him at all. All positive attributes are inadmissible with regard to God. If they are intended to mean anything real they are blasphemy; if nothing, a waste of breath.

This general conclusion is reinforced in the chapters on the 'negative attributes'.[1] Since we cannot describe positively what God is, the only thing left is to describe negatively what He is not. If the true idea is unattainable, we can at least get rid of the false. The idea of God has become as it were overlaid. If we would penetrate down to it, we must seek to remove the coverings under which it has been concealed. Granted that a complete knowledge is impossible, there are at least degrees in ignorance; the more we can free ourselves from errors, the more adequate becomes our comprehension. But the 'errors' and the 'mistakes' and the 'coverings' are precisely the vulgar opinions of Divinity which have been crystallized in the attributes of the theologians; it is then through the negating of those attributes that we proceed towards the knowledge of God. If we can prove that a certain attribute cannot be ascribed to God, then by that very negation we draw nearer to Him. Indeed it is only by negating a conventional attribute in this way that we draw near to Him at all. The logical end of the process is clear. The ideal is to negate every possible attribute ascribable

[1] I, caps. 58–60. It is sometimes forgotten that this famous doctrine, however strongly influenced later by Neo-Platonism, is derivable directly from the Hebrew Scriptures.

to God—negate, of course, by definite proof, not by mere verbal assertion. But if we finally succeed in negating every attribute, we may well ask, what have we left at all. Not only can we not describe what God is, but we must define Him by the very negation of description. The conclusion of the whole matter would seem then to be that God is pure negation, not only non-describable, but non-existent.

God as 'necessary existent'. (*a*) *Maimonides.* It is the characteristic view of Maimonides that this consequence does not follow. As we shall have occasion to point out later,[1] and as indeed is obvious from the whole trend of the discussion, it is only a certain type of attribute, the false positive of the imagination, which is inapplicable to God. That human descriptions are inadequate to express the nature of God does not mean that God has no nature. When we deny that the human mind can know what God is, we are reasserting the fact that God is non-human ; but each negation of inadequate conceptions of God's being reaffirms the fact that He exists. Existence in the case of God is not an accident ; it is identical with His essence. The more we negate the attributes the more we affirm the essence, and we are left finally with the idea of God as absolute existence. That God exists, therefore, and exists in the absolute sense that His very essence is existence, is the end of the whole discussion.[2] The first brush with the theologians is over. In place of a Godhead divided within itself according to the fancies of men, we have established the bare absolute existent of which existence is so essential an aspect as to be its very essence. And this conclusion is repeated in many places and in many forms. As a conclusion it may be invalid, but it shares its invalidity with the *causa sui* of

[1] p. 136.

[2] Cf. Kaufmann, *op. cit.*, p. 471 ; and *Guide*, e. g. I, cap. 57, p. 80 ; cap. 52, p. 71 ('God has absolute existence while all other beings have only possible existence') ; cap. 63, p. 95 (on the Tettragrammaton) ; II, cap. I, p. 152–3 (third and fourth philosophical arguments, with reference to props. 19–20, p. 147).

Spinoza. The one as much as the other stands or falls by the argument that if there is anything existing at all, then there is a 'necessary existent'.

(*b*) *Spinoza.* We have seen already that this is the argument for the existence of God as it assumed shape in the mind of Spinoza, as distinct altogether from the 'ontological' argument advanced by Descartes. It is interesting however to note that this essential divergence was remarked by no less a man than Leibniz. It will be remembered that the arguments for the existence of a Being 'whose essence involves existence' were made the subject of a special inquiry from Spinoza by one of his philosophizing friends.[1] Some ten years after, Leibniz sought out Spinoza at the Hague and submitted to him a very similar, if not identical, line of reasoning. Now at the end of his statement of this argument there is inserted a scholium in which the Cartesian argument from idea to existence, as opposed to his own (and Spinoza's) from existence of one kind to existence of another, is declared to be invalid, on the ground that any argument from idea is open to the objection of possessing a personal authority only.[2] For this reason, which we showed earlier to be justified, he prefers the form that avoids any suspicion of subjectivity: 'A being the essence of which is existence necessarily exists; God is a being whose essence is existence; therefore God necessarily exists.'[3] Of this reasoning, he tells us, Spinoza approved, a fact not to be wondered at, seeing that it is Spinoza's own. But when we say that it is Spinoza's own, we must not forget that it appears again and again in the pages of Maimonides. True, it cannot be proved that it was from Maimonides that Spinoza took over this conception. It was not uncommon in scholastic thought,[4] and there is no reason why it should not have come to Spinoza through the direct study of the scholastics. In this connexion

[1] *Epp.* XXXIV–VI; cf. above, p. 57 n. 2.
[2] See the text quoted above, p. 38 n. 2.
[3] Ap. Stein, *Leibniz und Spinoza*, pp. 98–9.
[4] Ib., p. 91.

however it is important to remember a curious fact about the scholastic movement itself. From the beginning of the thirteenth century, that is, from the time of William of Auvergne and Alexander of Hales downward, few single books seem to have exercised a greater formative influence upon the thought of the great churchmen than the *Guide for the Perplexed,* and many fundamental views, transferred bodily from the *Guide,* found a lasting home within their systems of philosophic theology.[1] Now, one of the opinions of Maimonides which found acceptance in the work of Aquinas was precisely that under discussion: the illegitimacy, namely, of ascribing any attribute but that of existence to God, who alone in the contingent world is possessed of absolute existence. Not the trend of the argument only but the very words are reproduced; and the doctrine, which in one place is given dogmatically as Aquinas' own, is given in another in the name of Maimonides.[2]

[1] See Guttman's essay *Der Einfluss der maimonidischen Philosophie auf das christliche Abendland* in the first volume of *Moses ben Maimon*; and *Ueberweg-Heinze,* ii [10] (Berlin, 1915), e. g. p. 468 (Maimonides and Albert); pp. 494, 496–8 (Maimonides and Aquinas).

[2] See the quotations from *Contra Gentil.* I, caps. 12 and 22, and *Quaest. disput. De Potentia Dei,* qu. 7, art. 2, given in Guttmann's essay, p. 180 (e. g. 'ipsum divinum esse est sua essentia seu natura'; '*Rabbi Moyses* dicit, quod Deus est ens non in essentia et vivens non in vita et potens non in potentia et sapiens non in sapientia; ergo in Deo non est aliud essentia quam esse' . . . &c.) The third argument of Aquinas for the existence of God, drawn 'ex possibili et necessario', and based on the proposition that 'Si omnia sunt possibilia non esse, aliquando nihil fuit in rebus; sed si hoc est verum, etiam nunc nihil esset'; is derived immediately from Maimonides (third philosophical argument, II, cap. i, p. 152). The text (from Summa I, 2. 3) is given in Krebs, *Thomas von Aquin, Texte zum Gottesbeweis* (*Kleine Texte,* Marcus und Weber, 1912), p. 55.

§ 4. *The Cosmological Problem: The Structure of the Universe*

The fundamental character of the issue involved in the attribute problem comes into clearer light when we turn to the consideration of the created universe. The reduction of the many to the one in knowledge is real only if the one is real. The unity must not be manufactured out of the diversity but found in it, and found not as a verbal postulate only. In theological language the quarrel is between monotheism and polytheism. To a polytheism there is no truth, only truths, truths disjoined from one another except under the artificial and contested sovereignty of the dynasty reigning in heaven. To a monotheism all the diversity of phenomena are only different expressions of the one law.

The theologians, so Maimonides tells us, were fully alive to the importance of the proper understanding of the relations between God and the universe, but this for a purpose and in a way of their own. It seemed to them that some form of the cosmological argument, the argument, that is, drawn from the structure of the universe as created, was the only way whereby the existence of God could be established. But they thought that the more perfect and orderly the universe, the less need would there be for it to have a creator. The greater the exercise of power therefore which could be shown to be necessary for the maintenance and continued order of the universe, the more cogently would the actual presence of order argue to the existence of God. If the constitution of the universe in itself could be shown to be the very denial of order, then they considered that it would be legitimate to argue that what order we as a fact experience is due to the constant intervention of a power from outside the universe, i. e. God. To the establishment of this premiss, then, namely that in the physical constitution of the universe taken by itself there is no order or continuity, the theologians devoted all their energies.[1]

The physical propositions assumed for the purpose of constructing the stage for this theophany are presented in the seventy-third chapter of the *Guide*, a chapter which, in view of its contents, it is not surprising that Leibniz took the trouble to summarize.[2] They turn generally upon the theories of the atomists, theories which, as Maimonides grimly remarks, were found by the theologians most convenient for the achievement of their ends.[3] The atomistic conception however is applied to other than physical entities. Wherever continuity might be held to exist, there the atoms are enthroned, in order that the observed continuity might indicate the presence of the direct action of God. ' Things ' are collections of atoms which would fall apart from one another but for the intervention of God. Space is a collection of space atoms, divided by a vacuum ; motion therefore is an accident, due to the direct action of God. Time is composed of time atoms, the universe then would not exist for more than the period of one of them, but for the conservation of God. Difference in substances is due not to difference in the composing atoms but to their created accidents, accidents which in every atom of time need

[1] The method of the ' Kalam ' is often criticized, particularly in I, cap. 71. For the word ' Kalam ', Bloch (in *Moses ben Maimon*, vol. i, p. 2 n. 1) quotes De Boér's *History of Philosophy in Islam :* ' An assertion expressed in logical or dialectic fashion, whether verbal or written, was called by the Arabs—generally, but more particularly in religious teaching—a Kalam (λόγος), and those who advanced such assertions were called Mutakallimun. The name was transferred from the individual assertion to the entire system. . . . Our best designation for the science of the Kalam is "Theological Dialectics", or simply "Dialectics"; and . . . we may translate Mutakallimun by Dialecticians ' (trans. E. R. Jones : Luzac & Co., 1903, pp. 42–3).

[2] *Leibniz, la philosophie juive et la Cabale*, pp. 12–16.

[3] I, cap. 71, p. 109. Stein notes the ' Mephistophelian irony ' of the theists' taking refuge with Democritus (*Archiv für die Geschichte der Philosophie*, 1898, p. 332).

recreation in the recreated substance by the providence of God. The very absence of a property in a substance is a special creation; not only then all positive but all negative determinations as well are due to the immediate action of God. The universe being thus constituted, it is not difficult to demonstrate the existence of God.

The central proposition of this system of theological physics is the sixth, that dealing with the 'creation of the accidents'. The character of the substance depends not on anything inherent in itself, but on the created accidents, no one of which is granted an existence of longer duration than that of one atom of time. It follows that continuity does not exist in the substance but depends on a recreation of its accidents; since however there is no 'natural force' at all in the substance, it is just as possible that new accidents might be created for it, and attached to it, as that the old should be recreated. But just as there is no continuity within the bounds of the individual substance, so within the universe as a whole there are no links or connexions. Causation collapses immediately. Whatever new accidents come into being are due to no action but that of God. That the movement of the pen is followed by the appearance of tracings on the paper is no proof that the tracings were caused by the ink on the pen. The very movement of the pen is due to a special creation, distinct entirely from the creation of marks on the paper which is itself of course a continuously new creation; and the exactness of the temporal correspondence is proof of nothing but the omnipresent care of the providence of God. The very will of man, according to one prevalent opinion, is only a collection of volitions each one of which is a special creation. And as the will so the knowledge. 'According to this principle—the theory of the "creation of the accidents"—the knowledge which we have of certain things to-day, is not the same which we had of them yesterday; that knowledge is gone and another like it has been created. They positively believe that this does take place, knowledge being an accident. In like manner it would follow that the soul, according to those who believe that it is an accident, is renewed each moment in every animated being, say, a hundred thousand times; for as you know, time is composed of time atoms. . . . There does not exist anything to which an action could be ascribed; the real agent is God . . .' [1]

That this extraordinary theory is only the logical outcome of a voluntaristic theism we have already seen. The problem of continuity is one of the fundamental issues on which sides must be taken; and if a theism is to be merely creational then there is only one side which the theist may adopt.[2] To put time or motion into the universe, it would seem, is to surrender to materialism. Nor can there be permanent essences in the universe apart from the will of God. If the world may be supposed to go on without God then the hypothesis of God would be superfluous. But God exists; and therefore (and herein Descartes and Gassendi in the seventeenth century are in full accord with the Arabic theologians of the twelfth) [3] any idea of permanence must be swept away from the universe as such.

To Maimonides, as to Spinoza, this whole train of thought is fundamentally unsound. It is not true that the presence of order within the universe precludes the presence of an ordering intelligence outside the universe. On the contrary the more we can find of the former, the more we become convinced of the latter. The objection to the theory of the theologians is not that they premise the efficient causality of God, but that through a misunderstanding of the nature of that causality they reduce the universe of knowledge to a chaos.

[1] I, cap. 73, p. 125.

[2] 'Materia enim quiescens quantum in se est, in sua quietate perseverabit, nec ad motum concitabitur *nisi a causa potentiori externa*. (Spinoza, *Ep.* LXXXI); cf. *S.T.* I, cap. ii, p. 30, l. 18 f.

[3] Some remarks on this coincidence are to be found in Mabilleau, *Histoire de la philosophie atomistique* (Alcan, 1895), p. 399, and in Stein's article in his *Archiv* (1898), p. 334.

In a world in which anything may happen knowledge is impossible; but it is only through knowledge of the world that we can know God at all. The founding of the argument for the existence of God on an intellectual scepticism is therefore a logical contradiction; or to express the same thing in theological language, a blasphemous mockery.[1]

Monotheism in Maimonides. That they will not allow a permanent order to the universe is then the fundamental objection of Maimonides to the philosophy of the theologians.[2] From the existence of chaos one can deduce only a chaos of source, but if we admit a universal chaos, then knowledge becomes unattainable. The objection to the theological doctrine of essential attributes is, as we saw, that it leads to a polytheism; but the objections to a polytheism are more than verbal or theological. The unity of God has a deeper significance than that of a mere dogmatic affirmation. It is the essential premiss in the pursuit of knowledge. The pursuit of knowledge presupposes a real unity in Nature; and the unity of Nature springs out of the unity of God. The very variety in the

[1] 'Such is, according to their opinion, the right interpretation of the creed that God is the *causa efficiens*. But I, together with all rational persons, apply to those theories the words: Will ye mock at Him as ye mock at man?' (*Guide*, I, cap. 73, p. 126.) That God can only be known through a study of the physical principles of the universe is affirmed repeatedly, e. g. I, cap. 34, p. 45: 'We can only obtain a knowledge of Him through His works; His works give evidence of His existence, and show *what must be assumed* concerning Him.'

[2] 'The Mutakallemun establish their arguments on propositions which are to such an extent *contrary to the actual state of things* as to compel these arguers to *deny* altogether the existence of the *laws of nature.*' I, cap. 71, p. 112. 'The Mutakallemun do *not hold that the Universe has any defined properties* on which a true proof could be founded, or that man's intellect is endowed with any such faculty as would enable him to form correct conclusions.' I, 75, p. 141. The concluding section of Part I contains a warning drawn from the 'fate of these speculators' who 'weakened the argument for the existence of God' by '*denying the nature of existing things and misrepresenting the properties of heaven and earth*'. (Cap. 76, p. 144.)

universe adduced by the theologians in support of their doctrine of essential attributes tells against them ; for variety is no sign of chaos but of the intimate interworking of things.[1]

In the same spirit therefore as Maimonides rejected the theological doctrine of essential attributes and set up that of the pure unity of God, so he dismissed the physical theory of the atomistic discreteness of things and set up that of the unity of nature. 'This universe in its entirety', he affirms in the impressive chapter inserted immediately before the discussion of the Kalam, 'is nothing else but one individual being ; that is to say, the outermost heavenly sphere, together with all included therein, is as regards individuality beyond all question a single being like Said and Omar. The variety of its substances—I mean the substances of that sphere and all its component parts—is like the variety in the substances of a human being . . . there is no vacuum whatever therein, but the whole space is filled up with matter . . . existing beings stand in relation to that sphere as a part of a thing stands to the whole . . .' It will be noted that Maimonides means by the universe not only the earth on which we live. It is the whole system of the spheres without cleavage or exception, i. e. the whole physical universe, which to his view is penetrated throughout with one order and obeys throughout one law.[2]

It is of the universe taken in this widest and most comprehensive sense that he asserts the essential parallelism of

[1] Cf. Kaufmann, *Attributenlehre*, pp. 395–6, n. 57 (contrast Munk, vol. i. p. 211, n. 2). The essential connexion between theological atomism and the theory of attributes is noted by Mabilleau, *op. cit.*, pp. 368–9.

[2] I, cap. 72. Cf. 'Tota natura naturata non [est] nisi unicum ens,' *Cog. Met.* II, 9, § 3 ; 'Totam naturam unum esse individuum', *Eth.* II, Lemma 7, sch. end ; 'Natura semper eadem et ubique una', III, pref. For the importance of this 'vision of all reality as one' in Spinoza's system cf. Sorley in *Proceedings of the British Academy*, 1917–18, p. 477.

universe with man. The point of the analogy lies in the fact that they are both organic wholes, composed of parts inextricably interconnected. 'It is impossible', he says, 'that any of the members of a human body should exist by themselves, not connected with the body, and at the same time should actually be organic parts of that body; that is to say, that the liver should exist by itself, the heart by itself, or the flesh by itself; in like manner it is impossible that one part of the universe should exist independently of the other parts in the existing order of things...'[1] This order, which arises from the fact of the complete interdependence of all things, Maimonides claims to be real, as opposed to the assumed order of the theologians. Indeed on the reality of this order he bases his whole metaphysic. It is on the premiss of the unity of nature—illustrated, not of course, as he is careful to note, proved, by the comparison with the human organism—that he argues for the existence of God. Whatever arguments are put forward rest on this premiss of unity, particularly the palmary argument from motion. Without the unity of nature, there is no proof of the existence of God; while it is from the existence of the one God that the unity of nature proceeds. The two are inseparable truths. The one God created one nature, and the one nature is created by the one God.[2] And of this one nature man is a part, an infinitesimal portion of the body of the vast organism—*quasi vermiculum in sanguine* as Spinoza expressed it[3] in the simile in which he embodied precisely the same idea in precisely the same way.

Pluralism in Descartes. There is then the closest possible connexion between a creational (or voluntaristic) theism and

[1] I, cap. 72, p. 115.

[2] 'He who is one has created only one being', ib., p. 115. 'We prove the unity of God from the fact that this universe is one whole', II, cap. 1, p. 154. For this famous theorem cf. II, cap. 22, first axiom, with Munk's note (vol. ii, p. 172 n. 1), and Steinschneider, *Hebräische Uebersetzungen*, pp. 22 and 244.

[3] *Ep.* XXXII.

an atomistic physics on the one hand and a logical theism and the doctrine of unity of substance on the other. In the discussion of the *causa sui* of Spinoza we had occasion to point out the distinction between the dynamical and logical aspects of the idea of cause.[1] It is now clear that this distinction divides not only Spinoza from Descartes but also Maimonides from the Kalam. The conviction of the logician that nature is a logical whole for the intellect, as opposed to the feeling of the voluntarist that nature, if it may be said to exist at all, is a collection of independent entities with the characteristics of individual wills, sums itself up in the doctrine adopted by Spinoza from Maimonides of the unity of nature, or the unity of substance. If we turn to the Cartesian doctrine of substance again, the point will be made more clear.

The self-conserving *causa sui* of Descartes is the unique substance which alone ' requires nothing but itself in order to exist '.[2] In the universe of efficient causes there is only one thing which has the power of self-conservation, but it does not follow therefrom that there is only one substance in the universe. Indeed the contrary must be insisted upon. If God's efficient causality were confined to Himself there would be no world at all. The very knowledge of the existence of God, however, depends for Descartes on the fact that apart from Him there is something else, within the mind of which the idea of Him is found. God in fact is only one (howbeit the most important one) among others. The existence of these others Descartes is forced to recognize under the name of created substances,[3] and however he may insist on their direct causal dependence on God their irreducible character becomes obvious in such an argument as that ' demonstrating ' the immortality of the soul.[4] Substance in the Cartesian meta-

[1] Above, pp. 58–61. [2] *Princ.* I, 51. [3] *Princ.* I, 52.

[4] Which rests on the statement that ' omnes omnino substantias . . . ex natura sua esse incorruptibiles '. (*Synopsis of Meditations*, p. 14, ll. 1–2.)

physic is in fact only another form of the 'discrete idea' of the logic or the 'simple nature' of the physics, and leads to a pluralism of 'independent reals' each one of which is 'really distinct' and 'can exist apart from the others'.[1]

Within this universe of discrete entities the fact of difference depends and can depend only on a difference of relation to the one immediate efficient cause. Now, this difference cannot arise from the entities themselves because they are completely and immediately dependent both for their essence and their existence on the primary cause. It follows therefore that any difference that exists can come only from the side of the cause itself. The supreme cause expends as it were different quantities of power in order to produce different things. All are immediate products of God's creative activity but some are more difficult to create or to conserve than others. Those which are more difficult to conserve are more real; those which are less difficult are less real. The most real of all is the Infinite which alone has power to maintain itself in existence; and from the Infinite downwards according

[1] Cf. the various definitions of substance, or rather substances. 'Nempe haec ipsa est notio substantiae, quod per se, hoc est absque ope ullius alterius substantiae, possit existere; nec ullus umquam qui *duas substantias* per duos diversos conceptus percipit, non iudicavit illas esse realiter distinctas' (*Resp.* IV, p. 226, ll. 3–7). '*Omnis res* cui inest immediate, ut in subiecto, sive per quam existit aliquid quod percipimus, hoc est aliqua proprietas, sive qualitas, sive attributum, cuius realis idea in nobis est, vocatur Substantia' (*Resp.* II, App., Def. V, p. 161, l. 14 f.). '*Duae substantiae* realiter distingui dicuntur cum unaquaeque ex ipsis absque alia potest existere' (ib., Def. X, p. 162, l. 11). The reduction of the created substances to two is arbitrary. Within 'thinking substance' individual souls retain independent existence; there seems no reason therefore why the same should be denied to the 'stone' of *Med.* III (p. 44, l. 18 f.) within the confines of 'extended substance'. The pluralistic premiss would seem to be prior to the denial of causality. If things are self-subsistent then any one can be thought of apart from any other, that is to say, no one thing depends on any other; the causal nexus therefore must be non-necessary.

to the ratio of the power needed for their conservation are ranged first the various other substances and then the modes. The doctrine of degrees of reality therefore in Descartes' system has no meaning outside of the doctrine of the transeunt causality of God. Indeed the two are to all intents and purposes identical, for the supreme case of degrees in reality is just that consciousness of the imperfection of the self from which is inferred the existence of omnipotence. The 'degrees' in fact are not degrees in any intelligible sense at all, because each distinct object refers back immediately to the supreme cause, the extent of the creative exertion alone of which is the index of the degree of reality of the product.[1]

Monism in Spinoza. In a 'universe which in its entirety is nothing but one individual being' the problem changes entirely. There is no longer any question of a pluralism, or the possibility of a pluralism. The monistic ideal in itself is the starting-point. The fact that Spinoza called the ultimate unity 'substance' is only another instance of his appropriation of the Cartesian terminology in a new sense. Or rather it would be more true to say that the whole stress of his doctrine is not on the word substance but on the use of it in the singular number. In the *rerum natura* there cannot be two or more substances, because the *rerum natura* is itself the one unique substance. The problem is not how many substances there are, or how their differences may be reconciled; but how, within the one substance, we may speak of substances at all.[2]

The question of the individuality of things would gain therefore no further light from the doctrine of degrees in the Cartesian sense. The immanent cause of a thing, to use the

[1] That there are 'degrees in reality' is an axiom (App., *Resp.* II, ax. 6). The criticism advanced is that of Spinoza himself (above, p. 59).

[2] Above, p. 56. This is true already of the *Short Treatise*; cf. Delbos, *Le Spinozisme*, p. 30

technical phrase of Spinoza, which after all means little more than the essential nature of that thing, cannot be spoken of as having exerted more power in the production of one thing than in the production of another. The details are overshadowed by the whole. Since the one substance comprehends all things, they are not to be considered as independent, owing allegiance only, and that directly, to the supreme, efficient cause. They are interlocked one with the other ; indeed, since individually they are each quantitatively less than all the others when considered together, they are severally more affected by the impress of all the others than by the enjoyment of their own active essence. Even assuming therefore the possibility of accepting the Cartesian doctrine of degrees with regard to what might be called their theoretical essence, from the practical point of view the doctrine would be useless ; because all things are what in practice they are, more through the essences of the other things with which they are interconnected than through their own.

How this fruitful thought points to its own solution in the developed system of Spinoza ; how indeed it is the very kernel of his whole ethical and metaphysical thought, will be shown later. It is sufficient so far to have indicated that in this as in so many other points of dispute with Descartes, Spinoza was following directly in the footsteps of Maimonides in his attack on the Kalam.

§ 5. *The Logical Problem : Knowledge and the Knowable*

The third great metaphysical problem discussed in the *Guide* is the logical (as opposed to the psychological) problem of knowledge ; the problem, that is, not how men get to know things but what there is in things that men get to know. To the theologian of course the problem does not exist. The higher mysteries cannot be known at all in any natural sense, what we do know being vouchsafed through a revelation ;

while the lower mysteries, those of the physical world, having no certainty in themselves, are no subjects for knowledge at all. That we are used to see things act in a definite way is no evidence that they will never act in any other; and since all things are ultimately of the same composition, anything may be expected to become anything else. A universe in which all things are the immediate products of a non-rational power is not a universe in which rational knowledge is possible. God so overshadows it that we could know nothing but Him; and His ways are *ex hypothesi* incomprehensible.

Against this point of view Maimonides directs all the weapons of his logic. For him as for Spinoza, God is anything but an *asylum ignorantiae.* His wisdom may not be as our wisdom, but that is because the mere fact of its all-comprehensiveness makes it different in kind from ours. The infinite intellect is not the reversal, but the completion, of the finite.[1] It is precisely the rationality of anything which is a proof of its divine origin; and the more rationality we find, the greater the vision we have of God. '"If you are asked whether this land has a king, you will undoubtedly answer in the affirmative." "What proof have you?" "The fact that this banker here, frail and insignificant in himself, stands before this large mass of gold pieces, and that poor man, tall and strong, who stands before him asking in vain for alms of the weight of a carob grain, is rebuked and is compelled to go away by the mere force of words; for had he not feared the king he would without hesitation have killed the banker or pushed him away and taken as much of the money as he could."'[2] The existence of order then is the proof that the country has a king; and the greater the evidence of order, the greater is the conviction that the king exists.

The place of God in the universe then is not that of the

[1] For the relation between the *intellectus archetypus* and the *intellectus ectypus* cf. below, p. 134, n. 1, end.

[2] *Guide*, I, cap. 46 (p. 59).

worker of miracle but that of the embodiment of law. It is only through insistence on and study of that law that we can know anything of God. And herein lies the great lesson of the *Guide* to the 'perplexed' of all ages. The religious man is not the man who turns his back on knowledge, but the man who is ever striving to know. The pursuit of knowledge is not only a possibility or a hardly won right; it is the one ethical duty: and it is an ethical duty because it is the aim put before man by religion. The religious life, according to the creed of Maimonides, is to learn what can be learned, 'to find a proof for everything which can be proved', to know what can be known, because it is only by and through the knowledge of the facts of the physical universe that we can claim to know anything of God. Such knowledge may be fragmentary and obscure, but it is the only knowledge which man can gain.

The difficulties involved in the working out of this point of view are nowhere illustrated more clearly than in the treatment of the problem of the origin of the world. The Aristotelians argued from the nature of the universe as it is now to the doctrine of eternity: motion and its varieties—time, and the facts of growth and dissolution, can have no beginning; therefore the universe is eternal. The perplexing character of the dilemma hereby presented to Maimonides is obvious. Pledged by all the forces of his intellectual nature against the chaotic scepticism of the theologians, he was yet loath to adopt the mechanistic materialism of the philosophers. But to deny the doctrine of eternity would seem to be equivalent to denying the universal validity of thought. If the laws of motion are valid now, surely they must be valid for all time. But if they were valid for all time in the past, they could have had no beginning; and if they are to be valid for all time in the future, they can have no end. The disjunction seems complete. The two contradictory views comprise the possibilities; and either a 'tychism' or a fatalism holds the day.

The consideration of this perennial problem, one of the great watersheds of human speculation, occupies the central portion of the *Guide*; and its resolution (to which in his correspondence he returns continually) is the nodal point of Maimonides' philosophy.[1] The detail of his general argument for a free cause cannot be discussed here, but attention must be directed to the peculiar character of his method of attack. He first destroys the position of the philosophers by pointing out the 'transcendental fallacy' of arguing from the nature of the world as it is to the nature of the world as it might once have been; as if a *philosophus autodidactus*, as he explains in a remarkable simile, reared by an animal on a desert island, could understand by a consideration of his present mode of life the facts of his pre-natal existence.[2] He then indicates the necessary inconclusiveness of any dogmatic statements about the origins of the universe of which we ourselves are a part. The arguments for and against the theory of creation, he says, present antinomies neither side of which compels assent. Hence the dogmatism of the philosophers is as unjustified as that of the theologians. On the one point then on which demonstration is impossible we may accept the opinion of the theologians, i. e. that the universe had a beginning. But to say that the universe had a beginning does not mean that there was a time when the universe was not, because time and with it the laws of motion have no existence apart from the universe. With the coming into being of the universe came time and motion, the 'accidents of matter'; and therefore it need give us no cause for surprise that in themselves they are eternal and yet were created. But to adopt the opinion of the theologians with regard to the origin of the universe

[1] II, caps. 13–25. There is a monograph on the subject by Rohner, *Das Schöpfungsproblem bei Moses Maimonides, Albertus Magnus und Thomas von Aquin* (*Beiträge zur Geschichte der Philosophie des Mittelalters*, xi, part 5).

[2] II, 17 (p. 179).

does not involve agreeing with them as to its nature. The constitution of the universe as created may, indeed must, be understood and investigated according to the method of the philosophers.[1]

That such in fact was the purpose of the whole argument is seen from Maimonides' treatment of the further question as to whether the universe will necessarily come to an end.[2] To the theologians the doctrine of creation involved the dogma of destruction ; because the caprice which brought the world into being and conserves it in being might just as easily resolve it again into nothingness. Now Maimonides is not only not bound to this conclusion, but is definitely pledged to reject it. His argument for the possibility of creation is framed specifically in order to meet the intellectual demand for a permanent order. Since the human mind is incapable of demonstrating that the world either had or did not have a beginning, it is legitimate to assume that it had a beginning. But now that it is in existence with universal laws, their very universality involves that it should continue for ever. The real contention of the philosophers therefore is not only conceded but reinforced. Although one cannot argue from the properties of a fully developed thing to its properties before it had attained that development, yet in its developed state these properties are necessarily permanent and inviolable. The former position was indeed advanced only in order to secure the latter. It was precisely Maimonides' conviction of the eternity of law that produced the original difficulty, and he is at no pains to conceal his own willingness to

[1] See the summary of the argument in II, cap. 16 ; and for 'time' e. g. II, cap. 13, pp. 171–2. The position which was to become so important in the Kantian philosophy that proof of the origin of nature cannot be found in nature is the point of the parable of the man reared in the island and is affirmed explicitly in e. g. II, cap. 23, p. 195 ('such a proof does not exist in nature ').

[2] II, caps. 27–8.

adopt the philosophical doctrine in its entirety, if otherwise the sacrifice of the conception of law were inevitable.

Now in the whole discussion a most important principle is at stake. Maimonides is concerned as we have seen not so much with the doctrine of creation as such as with the compatibility of the conceptions of God and law within the same universe. The concept of God belonged to the theologians; that of law to the philosophers. Maimonides' task really is then, as he himself says, to arrive at the conclusions of the theologians without giving up the method of the philosophers. In order to do this he points out that the conception of God is far from implying the absence of law in the universe; and that the conception of law is far from implying the absence of God. It is clear then that the crucial point of his position is precisely this connexion between law and God, the relation in fact between the will of God and the laws of nature. For our general inquiry the question is all-important, because, as it will be remembered, it was precisely on this point that the logic of Descartes gave final proof of its failure.

The Eternal Verities. It must be agreed that Maimonides is very far from bowing down to the idol of naturalism. The contemplation of a blind procession of matter and motion in their endless and unceasing combinations filled him with indignation and horror. Again and again he returns to the phrase 'will of God', and so lays himself open to the same charge of obscurantism as Spinoza makes against Descartes.[1] When we examine however the general trend of the polemic against the naturalistic philosophers, the significance of the appeal to the will of God becomes clearer. The objection to the mechanistic theory is not that it seeks to explain, but that it does not explain enough. Assuming certain data the mechanist can show the course of evolution, but what of the data themselves

[1] III, caps. 13 (particularly p. 274)—15; and 25 (particularly p. 308); cf. Husik, *Mediaeval Jewish Philosophy* (Macmillan & Co., 1918), pp. 273–6.

and the nature and origin of that course ? It is this gap in the mechanistic theory which leads Maimonides to the conception of a free creation, but the will of God invoked therein is not a substitute for, but the very ground of, rational explanation. The will of God and the wisdom of God are not, as the attributists insist, distinct aspects of Him, there being as it were one side of the Godhead which thinks and another which wills ; but will and wisdom are one with the very essence of God. When therefore we refer the nature of created things to His will, we mean by it not a non-rational caprice but an infinite and all-wise understanding. When from the *a posteriori* study of phenomena we deduce a physical law, it is always possible that our data have been insufficient or that we have been mistaken in our deduction. 'Law' is after all nothing but the simplest available verbal account of manifold data and has no validity beyond the data on which it was formed.[1] And this is finally the rational justification of Biblical, i. e. historical, miracles ; they are events, which, although unusual, are not less than others deep-rooted in the very heart of things.[2] The conceptions therefore of nature and natural law must be accepted with caution. To erect our small knowledge into an

[1] 'When a simple mathematician reads and studies these astronomical discussions, he believes . . . them . . . facts established by proof. But this is not the case. . . . The object of the astronomer is simply to find a hypothesis . . . which would require the least complicated motion, &c. . . .' II, cap. xi, p. 167. The history of the doctrine that the aim of hypothesis is *σώζειν τὰ φαινόμενα* is traced by M. Duhem (*Système du Monde*, ii, p. 68 f.). It is an important point in Spinoza [e. g. *Ep.* IX (to de Vries) and *Ep.* XIII, pp. 48 and 50] ; and the early statement in *D.I.E.* § 57 n. 2 seems to recall this very text of Maimonides : Idem etiam de hypothesibus intelligendum quae fiunt ad certos motus explicandum qui conveniunt cum coelorum phaenomenis, nisi quod ex iis, si motibus coelestibus applicentur, naturam coelorum concludent, quae tamen alia potest esse, praesertim cum ad explicandum tales motus multae aliae causae possint concipi.

[2] Cf. the quotations from older authorities in II, cap. 29, p. 210. (The view is evidently approved by Maimonides and was believed by his contemporaries to be his own.)

iron deity with the philosophers, one might perhaps sum up Maimonides' criticism, though a more excusable, is yet a no less dangerous, mistake than to deify our ignorance with the theologians.

Are there then no permanent laws of any kind whatever ? If there are not, then from the point of view of logic the search for knowledge is foredoomed to failure. Granting that natural law so-called is simply a 'saving of appearances', can we admit that our deepest intellectual convictions have no more lasting validity ? Maimonides realizes the importance of the problem and deals with it clearly and decisively. The validity he refuses to the 'laws' of nature he grants to the laws of mind. What the mind recognizes as self-contradictory he declares to be incompatible in the created universe, i. e. in the Creator. There are then within nature bounds which the Creator Himself cannot trespass, 'things', as he sums up 'according to each of the different theories', which are 'impossible, whose existence cannot be admitted and whose creation is excluded from the power of God.'[1] Of these things the very type is presented by the conclusions of the mathematical sciences, which, being the very clearest manifestation of human reason, must be considered to be inherent in nature and in God. The existence of such permanent impossibilities, however obnoxious to the creationists, must be accepted as part of the very nature of things. 'We do not consider it a defect in God that He does not combine two opposites in

[1] III, cap. xv, p. 280. This was a well-known 'error' of 'Rabbi Moyses'; cf. the curious treatise *De Erroribus Philosophorum* (dated the third quarter of the thirteenth century), cap. xii, § 9, ap. Mandonnet, *Siger de Brabant*[2], Louvain, 1908, vol. ii: 'Ulterius erravit circa divinam potentiam. Dicit aliqua esse Deo possibilia, aliqua non ; inter quae impossibilia narrat impossibile esse accidens sine subjecto ; et quosdam quos appellat separatos, quia dixerunt Deum hoc posse, dicit ignorasse viam disciplinalium scientiarum . . .' It is interesting to compare this with the passages of Descartes quoted above, p. 28, n. 1. Descartes might well have been one of these 'separati'.

one object, nor do we test His omnipotence by the accomplishment of any similar impossibility.' . . . 'We do not call a person weak because he cannot move a thousand hundredweights, and we do not say that God is imperfect because He cannot . . . make a square whose diagonal should be equal to one of its sides . . .'[1] The crowning perversion of the doctrine of the creational God is the substitution of a casual volition for eternal verities; and to this both Maimonides and Spinoza retort that it is only from the rejection of universal contingency and from reliance on human reason that we can speak of eternity, truth and God, at all.

§ 6. *Recapitulation and Prospect*

The results so far achieved may be summed up as follows:

Descartes. The logic of Spinoza far from being dependent on, and a development of, the logic of Descartes, is a conscious and definite presentation of precisely the opposite point of view. The discrete idea; the creational deity; the voluntaristic metaphysic; have been shown to lead to a scepticism in which proof has no meaning and knowledge no place. The ideal of freedom, if severed from that of law, leads inevitably to chaos; and the logic of Descartes allows this uncontrolled ideal of freedom to penetrate all spheres in turn from the individual thoughts of man to the volitional activities of God, as if the inherent defects of the first premiss might be rectified by allowing it an ever wider licence. The experiment, however, boldly and uncompromisingly carried out though it was, was foredoomed to failure. It reached its highest point in its transference, from the sphere of theological physics to that of logic, of the conception of God as conservational cause, but, being unable to deny of God the freedom which it affirmed of man, was forced to see the universal order within its reach collapse into a universal chance. Knowledge as a whole of connected ideas was shown finally to be impossible, because

[1] I, cap. 75, pp. 139 and 141.

the existence of connexions between one idea and another was, *ex hypothesi*, wanting.

Spinoza. Spinoza, consciously recognizing the necessity of this conclusion, and yet convinced of the universal character of knowledge and the universal validity of logic ; was bound by the nature of the case to put forward a different premiss. If the discrete idea cannot lead to knowledge and yet knowledge is possible, then we must find some other starting-point from which to set out on our search. On the one side are the individual ideas corresponding with the individual things ; on the other side the totality of knowledge, corresponding with the totality of things which can be known. If we start from individual ideas, we cannot, as the Cartesian attempt had shown, arrive at the totality of knowledge. There is left then the alternative of assuming the totality of knowledge and working down from it to the individual ideas. This alternative Spinoza adopted unconditionally in whatever sphere of thought he entered upon, and in logic, theology, and metaphysics, insisted on the primary conception of God not as non-rational will but as universal reason embodied in the oneness of *natura naturata*.

Maimonides. Since it was clear that the logic of Spinoza was entirely separate and distinct from that of Descartes, evidence was sought in the writings of Spinoza for the philosophical literature which formed the background of his thinking. The required clue was found in the *Tractatus Theologico-Politicus*, the composition of which interrupted that of the *Ethics*, and attention was directed to the *Guide for the Perplexed* of Maimonides on which the archaeological inquiries at least of the Treatise were acknowledged to rest. An examination of this work showed that it contains a discussion and refutation of precisely the same type of logical thought as received expression four centuries later in Descartes. The necessary existence of God and the irrelevance of anthropomorphic attributes ; the unity of God and the unity of nature ; the rationality of the universe and the power and duty of man to reason—such fundamental principles are put forward on every page of the *Guide* in definite and specific opposition to the creational metaphysic and sceptical logic of the Kalam. But both the one and the other, both criticism and reconstruction, are found in every page of Spinoza in specific opposition to Descartes. It is possible that Spinoza misunderstood and misinterpreted Descartes just as much as it is possible that Maimonides misunderstood and misinterpreted the Kalam. But sufficient evidence has been given that whatever other developments the Cartesian logic may have been capable of, whatever other aspects it may have exhibited ; this at least, the voluntaristic and sceptical, was that which was specifically recognized by Spinoza. And since this is so, it is not extravagant to believe that he drew his weapons of attack against it, as he may have learned its recognition and rejection, from the pages of Maimonides.

Maimonides and Spinoza : 'Memini olim legisse'. The difficulty in the way of the general theory on the data presented is derived from chronological considerations. It is not only in the *Ethics* and the *Theologico-Political Treatise* that we find the characteristics which we have learned to recognize as Maimonidean, but also, as we have seen, in the early treatises *On God and Man* and *On the Improvement of the Understanding.* If then the work of Maimonides came into Spinoza's hands only when he was preparing to produce the *Theologico-Political Treatise,* we have yet to explain how Maimonidean views are found in Spinoza at a period of his philosophical career preceding the composition of this *Treatise* by many years.[1]

On closer examination, however, this apparent difficulty is easily resolved. If Spinoza had not been accustomed to look on Maimonides as a living force, he could never have

[1] Particular points in the *Short Treatise* have been noted in Wolf's edition, e. g. pp. 167, 174, 176, 177, 189, 197, 198, 205, 232.

selected him for specific attack; and if we remember how seldom it is his custom to quote authors by name the numerous references to Maimonides in the *Treatise* and the fact that its crucial chapters are specifically devoted to the refutation of his opinions, are of notable significance. Indeed general considerations drawn from the supreme influence of Maimonides in Hebrew literature would be sufficient to antedate Spinoza's acquaintance with his views. In the sphere of speculative thought Maimonides' influence is supreme, comparable only with that of Kant in the fifty years following the publication of the *Critique of Pure Reason*.[1] This is true not only of the immediately succeeding generations, when Gersonides developed his opinions to their logical conclusion and Crescas brought them into greater prominence by his attacks;[2] but also of the

[1] I borrow the comparison from Grünfeld, *Lehre vom göttlichen Willen*, &c. (*Beiträge zur Geschichte der Philosophie des Mittelalters*, vol. vii, part 6), p. 63. Husik (*op. cit.*, p. 312) is even more positive; 'In the post-Maimonidean age all philosophical thinking is in the nature of a commentary on Maimonides whether avowedly or not.'

[2] Cf. below, p. 139 n. 1, on Spinoza's theory of immortality. The same comment applies to many of Spinoza's supposed borrowings from Crescas [latest discussions in Waxman, *Don Hasdai Crescas*, Columbia University Press, 1920]. Joel himself showed how the Maimonidean treatment of the most important point, that of the freedom of the will, prepared the way for Crescas and Spinoza (*Zur Genesis*, &c., pp. 54–8). That 'rewards and punishments, as the consequences of good and bad actions, are themselves part of the necessary order of things' (Pollock, *Spinoza*, p. 91) is a familiar idea enough (see Maimonides, *Heleq*, translated by Abelson in *J.Q.R.*, October 1906, and the references given in the *Responsum* of R. Tzevi Aschkenazi, translated in the *Chronicon Spinozanum*, vol. i); while the famous concluding proposition of the *Ethics*, as a comparison with *Ep.* 43 and *Theol-Pol.* 4, § 41, will show, is only a reminiscence of the hoary wisdom of Solomom. Spinoza's conception of infinite extension, as opposed to finite and divisible corporeality (below, p. 118), may come from Crescas; but it is more readily understood as a transference to the sphere of a metaphysical physics of Maimonides' doctrine of the infinite and indivisible unity of the Divine omniscience [e. g. *Guide*, III, 20], as is, indeed, directly suggested by *Princ. Phil. Cart.* I, 9 sch.

later work of countless thinkers of different schools, down to and beyond the Paduan Averroism of the Joseph ben Shem Tob from whom Spinoza quotes,[1] and the Renaissance Neo-Platonism of the Leone Ebreo whose *Dialoghi di Amore* he possessed.[2] And this influence is not restricted to philosophical literature. The great grammarian and biblical commentator David Kimchi refers with reverence to the rationalistic theories of the *Guide to Righteousness*, and Gersonides read them right into the text of the Bible itself.[3]

Maimonides himself did not confine his metaphysical opinions to his professedly metaphysical work. All his writings alike contain a definite presentation of what he considered to be their metaphysical basis, while the most important and characteristic of all, the great digest of Rabbinical law called the Strong Hand,[4] is prefaced by a simple and positive

In any case, Crescas is the type of anti-rationalist theologian against whom the *Guide* is one long polemic.

[1] *Theol-Pol.* V, § 48. The book Kebod Elohim is an exposition of selected portions of the *Nicomachean Ethics* of Aristotle.

[2] In a Spanish translation (*Lebensgeschichte*, p. 161, no. 22). Cf. the brilliant essay of Dr. Carl Gebhardt, *Spinoza und der Platonismus* in the first volume of the *Chronicon Spinozanum*, and Solmi, *Benedetto Spinoza e Leone Ebreo* (Modena, 1903). Leone Ebreo (=Leo Abarbanel, 1460–? 1530) repeats almost verbally e. g. Maimonides' doctrine of the unity of nature as the correlate of the unity of God (end of Dial. II); the intellectual rapture and divine kiss (beginning of Dial. III); the different opinions as to the origins of the world; the grades of knowledge ending in the prophecy of Moses; and the 'explanation' of the Paradise story (Dial. III). [Cf. the Hebrew version (Lyck, 1871), pp. 38 b; 41 a; 55 b–58 b; 65 b–66 a; 72 a; Latin version (Venice, 1564), pp. 160; 182; 245 f; 286–8; 316.]

[3] The notes to the *Tract. Theol.-Pol.* in which these are mentioned are not from Spinoza (see Gebhardt in Appendix to Fischer's *Spinoza* [5], p. 601); but he was in possession of the great Rabbinic Bible of Buxtorf (*Lebensgeschichte*, p. 160, no. 1) which contained them and from the introduction to which, reprinted from the Bomberg Bible, he derived most of the Talmudic quotations used in the *Theol.-Pol.*

[4] Quoted specifically, though at second hand, in *Theol.-Pol.* V, § 47, and by way of reminiscence in *Cog. Met.* II, 6, § 3. Its importance

account of his whole philosophy. This digest, and with it the earlier commentary on the Mishnah, which contains numerous excursuses on most points of philosophic interest, became within the lifetime of the writer indispensable adjuncts to the study of the Talmud, and the Talmud was, as is well known, the very centre of the educational tradition in which Spinoza grew up. This *a priori* suspicion that Spinoza could not have avoided meeting with the philosophical views of Maimonides in however indirect a fashion, is confirmed (if confirmation were needed), by a contemporary memoir [1] which tells us that, in the highest class of the school in which he received his education, the boys 'learned a portion of the Talmud every day . . . and discussed the decisions of Maimonides . . .' Even if Spinoza therefore could by some accident have escaped the reading of the *Guide* itself, he could not have avoided absorbing its philosophy in the very school compendium from which he derived his early training.

Fortunately, there is other and better evidence than suspicions or generalities. It may well have been, as is held by Kuno Fischer, that the vision opened up to Spinoza by the new thought of Descartes obliterated every trace of what he once learned as a boy; that is to say, even if it be allowed that as a boy he had learned anything of Maimonides. It may well have been; only we have the directest evidence possible that it was not, the evidence of nothing less than an explicit statement of Spinoza himself. It is curious indeed that such a piece of autobiographical detail should have escaped attention, when the most illegitimate conjectures based on the scantiest evidence have been gladly entertained. I refer to the note at the beginning of the fifteenth chapter of the *Tractatus Theologico-Politicus*, the crucial chapter in which

for the study of Spinoza has been indicated by Karl Pearson in his essay on Maimonides and Spinoza in *The Ethic of Free Thought* (2nd ed., Black, 1901), pp. 125–142.

[1] *Lebensgeschichte*, p. 210.

the relations of Theology and Philosophy are discussed. Here Spinoza quotes the opinions of a certain Rabbi Jehuda Alpakhar, who was in the opposite camp to Maimonides. The reference is obviously obscure and needs some apology. 'I remember,' says Spinoza in the note, 'having read this years ago—*olim legisse*—in a letter against Maimonides included among his *Responsa*.' The words *olim legisse* do not refer to a recent study, and as the *Responsa* of Maimonides are not among his own books, it is natural to suppose that his acquaintance with them goes back to his school days. But be that as it may, 'many years' before the composition of the *Theologico-Political Treatise* he was interested enough in Maimonides to read his *Responsa*, and the memory remained with him sufficiently strongly to make possible its reproduction in an astonishingly accurate form. There is no need to lay stress on the particular contents of the *Responsa*. They touch on most philosophical topics (among other matters) and treat them in the characteristic Maimonidean way, a way which is the subject of bitter attack in the 'letters written against Maimonides' after his death. The few words of Spinoza are sufficient to establish the point on which we are at present concerned to insist. His interest in and study of Maimonides goes back to a period of his life much anterior to the composition of his two great works. The reference to the *Guide* which gave the *Theologico-Political Treatise* its essential content was no new departure, but a fresh consideration of a point of view with which Spinoza had been acquainted from the very beginning of his intellectual life. It would be idle to lay stress upon a casual phrase, did not its very casualness suggest a wider significance. If we had to sum up our view of the relations between Spinoza and Maimonides in a few words, it would be difficult to find any more appropriate than *memini olim legisse*. It would appear that Spinoza's study of Maimonides controlled his later thought, in the sense that unconsciously he tested whatever came to his hand in accordance with the principles which he had learned once for all in the *Guide*. The very petulance of his tone against Maimonides, which is not unlike that of Aristotle when he has occasion to make mention of Plato, is that of a pupil over-anxious to vindicate his own originality by a carping depreciation of the master.

When therefore we propose to treat Maimonides and Spinoza together as representing in common a distinct and different orientation of thought from that of Descartes and the Kalam, we assert, not the identity of their philosophies in detail but the far deeper and more significant fact that the one provided the primary and permanent background of the other. That the universe as a totality is God could never have been affirmed by Maimonides ; in its crude form indeed this doctrine was expressly repudiated by Spinoza.[1] But that which they hold in common against the opposing school is the conception of the universe as a totality through which alone it is possible to know God. Whether the order demanded by the universal claims of the thinking mind be equated with God, as in the developed philosophy of Spinoza ; or whether outside and beyond this order there exists an immaterial intelligence, as argued by Maimonides—this question, however important from other points of view, is yet from the point of view of logic of no practical relevance.[2] It is from the one Nature that

[1] 'Me hic per Naturam non intelligere solam materiam eiusque affectiones' (*Theol.-Pol.* VI, § 10 n.) ; 'quod quidam putant, *Tractatum Theologico-Politicum* eo niti quod Deus et Natura, per quam massam quandam sive materiam corpoream intelligunt, unum et idem sint, tota errant via.' (*Ep.* LXXIII, p. 239.) The palmary argument of Maimonides for the existence of a non-corporeal Being distinct from the universe was that drawn from the fact of motion. This argument, which was taken over from Maimonides by Aquinas, is specifically dismissed in *Short Treatise*, I, cap. ii, p. 30.

[2] The issue between 'immanence' and 'transcendence' is therefore only apparent, and hence Sorley's chief criticism of Joel (*Mind*, O.S., V, p. 376) falls to the ground. It is not at all clear that Spinoza, or indeed any other thinker, effected a complete fusion between 'natura naturans' and 'natura naturata'.

we learn the one God; and the one God can only be interpreted in and through the one Nature. It was this fundamental metaphysical idea which Spinoza used with such consistency and such effect against the whole movement of the Cartesian logic, and it was this same fundamental metaphysical idea which was the mainspring of Maimonides' attack on the Kalam. It remains to show that the permanent impression made on Spinoza's mind by the study of the *Guide* extended far beyond general principles. The memory which retained the objections of 'Rabbi Jehuda Alpakhar' was not likely to lose the intimate doctrine of the master himself.

IV. MAIMONIDES AND SPINOZA

Introductory : The Problems of a Monistic Logic

IF the problem of the voluntaristic logics, as exemplified by Descartes, is how from the particular to arrive at a whole ; then the problem of the intellectualist logics is how from the whole to arrive at the parts. To the one it is the induction of the infinite which is the difficulty ; to the other the deduction of the finite. To explain the existence of the finite is, of course, impossible. Such is the fact of nature, or, as Maimonides phrased it, the will of God ; and it would be no more use asking why the infinite has expressed itself in the finite than to ask why a square does not possess the properties of a circle, or why the details of a ceremony are not other than in fact they are.[1] The 'why' is, however, distinct from the 'how'. If we ask 'why', we can only say 'Quia ei non defuit materia' ;[2] but if we ask 'how', we are asking not for the reasons of the existence of the finite, which only a mind outside of the finite system could grasp ; but for the way in which the various finite entities group themselves together, and by this grouping produce the characteristic features of the finite world.

The answer to this second question, the question 'How ?' is found readily in, and indeed springs immediately out of, the original premiss. If Nature is one, then whatever is, is a part of Nature, and from this fact all human problems arise. The clash and disharmony in practical life, which produce all the phenomena of evil ; the conflicts and insufficiency of intellectual life which are the source of the phenomena

[1] Spinoza, *Ep.* LXXVIII, p. 251, and *Guide*, III, cap. 26, p. 311.

[2] *Eth.* I, Appendix (end) ; cf. *Guide*, III, cap. 25 : 'The Creator's intention was to give existence to all beings whose existence is possible' (p. 309).

of error; all arise from the fact that in one way or another, man, refusing to recognize his finite character, seeks to arrogate to himself the privileges of the infinite. Knowledge (and it is in the problem of knowledge that the question arises most vividly) is not for 'parts' of Nature, but only for Nature itself. To understand things as in reality they are, we should have to be as God is. But, since man is not God, complete understanding is for him an impossibility. We are, however, men, and our interests lie with the finite. It becomes, then, precisely the problem of ethics to show how the infinite may be brought into the finite life, or how, from the other point of view, the finite may be brought to recognize its place in and relation to the infinite. And so we have the curious paradox that both Maimonides and Spinoza, who alike, and with the most uncompromising frankness, deny categorically the absolute validity of moral values,[1] yet devote all their energies to the investigation of what is good for man. Since however, goodness is not in God (because it is absurd to suppose that God has aims outside of Himself), nor again in man (because man is a natural being, part of a Nature which knows nothing of final ends); [2] it can only lie in the relation between the two, consisting, indeed, primarily in the recognition of that relation and in the deepening of its understanding.[3] The doctrine that man is a part of Nature, therefore, is the essential

[1] e. g. *Short Treatise*, I, cap. 10; *Eth.* IV, pref. and 64 cor.; *Guide*, I, cap. 2 (from which the 'explanation' of the Paradise story in *Eth.* IV, 68 sch., is taken bodily, cf. Pollock, *op. cit.*, pp. 251–2). 'Ulterius erravit [Maimonides],' remarks the author of the *De Erroribus Philosophorum* (*loc. cit.*, § 12), 'circa humanos actus, ponens fornicationem *non esse peccatum in iure naturali.*'

[2] Above, cap ii, § 2, p. 49, § 3, p. 60 (for Spinoza); below, cap. iv, § 6, p. 136 (for Maimonides).

[3] 'Probi, hoc est, [ii] qui claram Dei habent ideam . . . improbi, hoc est, [ii] qui Dei ideam haud possident.' *Ep.* XXIII, p. 106, cf. *Ep.* XIX end. 'Those who have succeeded in finding a proof for everything that can be proved, who have a true knowledge of God so far as a true knowledge can be attained, and are near the truth wherever

complement to the doctrine that Nature is one. And just as the latter springs from the conviction of the unity and validity of knowledge, so the former works itself out into an ethical system only in and through the conviction of the attainability of knowledge. There is in fact from the absolute point of view no such thing as good and evil, only true and false; and such meaning as we can give to ethical right and wrong is to be sought through the gateway of a theory of logic.

§ 1. *The Problem of Error in Spinoza. Intellect and 'Imaginatio'*

The partial knowledge of the finite is called by Spinoza *Imaginatio*. The meaning of the words 'finiteness' and 'part' is illustrated in the well-known simile of the 'worm in the blood' contained in a letter to Oldenburg, and is defined with more professedly scientific exactness in the excurcus on physics in the second book of the *Ethics*.[1] Its importance in Spinoza's general philosophical outlook is evident from the many times he refers to it.[2] For our purpose it is necessary to show that the part it plays is not an insignificant or incidental one, but that it penetrates deep into every department of his thought; so deeply, indeed, that if it be taken away his whole metaphysic would become incoherent, and fail as an account of the world in which we live.

The self-dependent existent of which alone being may be predicated, which we have seen to be the centre of Spinoza's system, may be considered from four aspects, two absolute or infinite, two partial or finite. From the absolute aspect it is that which completely is, and that which completely is

an approach to the truth is possible, they have *reached the goal*.' *Guide*, III, 51 (p. 385).

[1] *Ep.* XXXII; *Eth.* II, Lemma 7 sch., inserted between props. 13 and 14.

[2] e. g. *S.T.* II, cap. 18, p. 115, and cap. 24, p. 140; *Cog. Met.* II, 9, § 3; *Tr. Pol.* II, § 5; *Theol.-Pol.* III, § 9, IV, § 3; *Epp.* XXX, XXXII; *Eth.* IV, 2–4, and App., caps. i, 6–7.

known; from the finite aspect it is that which is, and is known, more or less, and that with reference to which man is, and knows, more or less. We may summarize the characteristics of these aspects somewhat as follows:

To be is to be-one, and there is only one One. It is only the whole which, in the full sense of the word, is. This whole which is, is under infinite attributes in infinite ways, the whole being a system, not an agglomeration. A 'part'—if one can speak of a part, and strictly one cannot—only 'is' *in* the whole. Its essence or reality lies in this inherence.

This whole or totality of being is God as Reality, *deus sive natura.*

To be is to be-for-thought; 'essence' is 'objective' in 'idea'. But just as to be can be predicated only of the One as a whole, so to be-known can be predicated only of the One as a whole. Knowledge of a part as a part is not knowledge. Knowledge is of essence, and essence is inherence in the whole.

This ideal of Knowledge, the reflection of the ideal of Being, is God as Known, i. e., God as He knows Himself, or God as *intellectus.*

Within the whole there are partial 'points of view'. What we call 'finite' things are points of view of the whole, parts torn from their context. The more detached they are, the less they may be said to be; the more closely knit, the more they may be said to be. To be 'closely knit' in the whole is to hold a place which cannot be interchanged with any other, i. e., to be completely individual; and to be thus completely individual is to possess (or be possessed by) the whole in an unique and essential way. Such a finite thing torn from the context of the whole is man. To his 'point of view' therefore (viewing it for the moment statically), things (including of course himself) may be said to 'grow into' being and knowledge, that is, to be apprehended more and more as a manifestation of the whole.

God is here (from the point of view of man) the *intelligibile,* that which becomes known, or that which progressively is.

But man too, like other finite things, may knit himself further into the context of the whole. The more he knows, the more he is. The more he knows of the essence of things (himself included), the more essential a place he takes within the whole as Being and Known. Indeed by self-affirmation through knowledge he can attain the elevation at which it is all one to say that man thinks God or God thinks Himself in man.

This progressive clarification, as it were, of the mind of man, is, therefore, God as *intelligens*—that which gradually becomes knowing.

We have then the fourfold view of the whole or God, as Being, as Known, as growing-into-being, and as growing-into-knowledge.[1] From the point of view of human life, clearly the last two are the more important, and it was to throw light on them and their relation to the first that the treatise *On the Improvement of the Understanding* was composed. If we follow its argument, we may see the way in which Spinoza arrived at the thought which in its perfected form is presented in the *Ethics*.

The 'verum bonum et sui communicabile', he tells us, which alone can give complete emotional satisfaction, and which must be eternal and infinite in order that all can share in it without rivalry or pain, is the 'knowledge of the union which mind has with the whole of nature'. It can be attained, however, 'only if we deliberate on the matter thoroughly', and therefore all our powers must be concentrated on method.[2] That there is such a *summum bonum* cannot be doubted; indeed, it is demanded by the very nature of our mind.[3] The problem is, how it can be known. We are led to consider the

[1] The significant references are *Eth.* II, 7 sch., and II, 11 cor.

[2] *D.I.E.*, §§ 1–16.

[3] § 42; cf. §§ 47–8 and *Eth.* IV, 36 sch.: 'non ex accidenti sed ex ipsa natura rationis oriri ut hominis summum bonum omnibus sit commune, nimirum quia ex ipsa humana essentia quatenus ratione definitur, deducitur.'

various types of knowledge and their several values and methods.[1]

The highest of the forms of knowledge is *per solam essentiam rei* ; its instrument, the clear idea. Truth needs no sign. It is not the understanding of the causes of a thing *ab extra*, but the apprehension of the internal quality, the essence, by virtue of which it is. Reality and knowledge are the same thing. The real is the known, the most real—the *ens perfectissimum*—the most known. Knowledge and reality are inseparable, and just as reality is independent of the external, so is the knowledge of reality. That which is known is real : that which is real is known.[2]

But if to be known is to be real, how can there be such a thing as error ? If the real as a complete whole is, and is for knowledge ; then as everything that is, is real, so everything that is known is true. But then there cannot be such a thing as doubt, error, or fiction. Thought is identical with Being ; to be-in-thought is to be. Within the real and within the real-as-known, i. e., within the knowledge of the real, everything eternally must be and is. Mistake or fraud is impossible. Probability has no significance beyond our ignorance. If it had, life would be chance, and Science, with the 'happiness' which it brings, a cheat.

We can now understand the peculiar insistence of Spinoza on the *idea ficta* and the problem of possibility. It occupies the very first section of the first part of 'the method'. If thought is the same as Being, fiction cannot be the product of thought, because if it could we should have to admit that the chimaera or any other absurdity exists, i. e., predicate of reality that which is inconsistent with it. And if we are going to allow fictions (i. e., thought 'unreal' in some way)

[1] §§ 18–29.

[2] §§ 35–8 and §§ 69–70. Cf. *Eth.* II, def. 4 and 29 sch. ; and I, 30 sch. ('id quod in intellectu objective continetur debet necessario in natura dari').

to be affirmed indiscriminately, we cannot prevent 'real' thought being denied indiscriminately. And indeed so we find it to happen with regard to the supreme case. That God exists is the first and eternal truth. But men have doubted God's existence, because they have not understood what is meant by God: 'they feign something they call God which is not in harmony with the nature of God.' Hence it is the inability to distinguish fiction from truth that has led to the denial of the first and eternal truth which is the basis of all knowledge. It is therefore of fundamental importance to discover the origin of fiction and to distinguish it from truth.[1]

As a preliminary we must dismiss a current theory—that of the Cartesians. There is no such thing as a freely creative 'faculty of fiction' which 'by its own power creates sensations or ideas which do not belong to things' as if it were a 'kind of indeterminate God'.[2] Such an explanation would be worse than useless, for how should we be able to distinguish such fictions from true ideas? The truth is that fiction *is* a product of thought. In a sense it does 'belong to' things; and there is no harm in it so long as we recognize in what way it does so belong. It is not a 'simple' idea containing naturally the 'reflection' of its object, but an artificial composition of fragments, as it were, thrown together confusedly. 'It never makes anything new or affords anything to the mind; . . . only such things as are already in the brain or imagination are recalled to the memory . . . For example, speech and tree are recalled to the memory at the same time, and when the mind confusedly attends to both without distinction, it thinks of a tree speaking.'[3]

This explanation, however, only opens the door to a far greater difficulty. 'Thought is responsible for fiction'; but if so, of what value is thought? We start with the assumption

[1] §§ 50–4 with Spinoza's notes: cf. *Eth.* II, 47 sch. 'Possibility' is discussed in *Cog. Met.* I, caps. 1 and 3, and *Eth.* I, 33 sch.

[2] § 59–61.

[3] § 57, n. 1: cf. *Eth.* II, 47 sch.

that thought can, and will, bring us to truth, but are now faced with the fact that it brings us to error. And here the peculiar difficulty of Spinoza's general position is revealed. In order to account for error, he is pledged not to call in the will; but if he does not call in the will, it would seem that he must sacrifice the universal validity of thought. But if he sacrifices the validity of thought, he relinquishes the very core of the whole system. He is therefore bound by the very nature of the case to find a non-intellectual origin for the ideas which bear no guarantee of truth. The solution is given in the concluding section of the first part of the treatise. We learn that the ideas in question arise from the *imagination* 'as affected by individual and corporeal things', and that the imagination is definable as 'certain fortuitous and unconnected sensations . . . which do not arise from the power of the mind, but from external causes, according as the body, sleeping or waking, receives various motions'.[1] The conditions of error then are individual bodily images brought together 'fortuitously', i. e., not in accordance with the order of the mind; and their composition into the false idea is due not to the will of the individual, but to the determining influence of environmental facts.

If we follow out this conception, we see how it harmonizes with its general philosophical context. The sensations which make up the imagination arise from 'external causes'; but since everything proceeds from God, the external causes too must have a 'thought side' in Him. But if so, our thought, which sees them as external, can be only a partial manifestation of the thinking of God. Hence what is the corporeal imagination and the corporeal order to the individual man, is really the manifestation of God through other men or things.[2]

[1] §§ 82–4.

[2] 'Si de natura entis cogitantis est, uti prima fronte videtur, cogitationes veras sive adaequatas formare, certum est *ideas inadaequatas ex eo tantum in nobis oriri*, quod *pars sumus alicuius entis cogitantis*

But the order of God is the 'order of the mind'. In so far, therefore, as a man can transmute the order of the imagination into the order of the mind, that is, cease to be a merely 'passive' recipient of sensation; he is so far understanding things as God, achieving the 'union with the order of nature as a whole' which is the goal of the efforts of man. We have here, then, in the logical treatise, and as a direct consequence of the problem presented by the fact of error, and more particularly the fictitious idea, the whole doctrine of the *Ethics* with regard to the adequate or internally-self-dependent, and inadequate or externally-dependent, ideas, with its fundamental distinction between the order of the mind and the order of sense presentation,[1] which is nothing less than the world of things and human beings in which we live.

For our purpose it is important to emphasize the general nature of the solution offered. Man errs because he is not all thought; and he is not all thought because thought is something bigger than he, and works not only through him, but through other men and things as well. This 'inverted' thought, as it were, is what Spinoza calls imagination, and it owes its origin to the physical fact that man is only a part of the whole, and a part which is worked upon strongly by the other parts. If we turn to the argument, it is clear that its pivot is the opposition between imagination and intellect. It is with regard to the *imagination* that the soul is passive, not active, as it is in thought. It is the *imagination* which produces the conventional and dangerous errors that extension must be local and finite. It is because things which we easily *imagine* are clearer to us that our vocabulary is misleading (being framed to suit the *imagination*), and we find negative

cuius quaedam cogitationes ex toto, quaedam ex parte tantum, nostram mentem constituunt.' § 73: cf. *Eth.* II, 11 cor. and 28 dem.

[1] § 91; cf. e. g. *Eth.* II, 10 sch. 2; 18 sch.; 26 cor.; 29 sch.; IV, 4 and dem.; V, 10; V, 39 dem.; and *Ep.* VI, where the order of 'natura in se' is opposed to that of 'natura prout ad sensum humanum relata' (pp. 22 and 25).

names bestowed on what are really positive ideas, and positive names on what are really negative ideas. It is to the *imagination*, therefore, that we owe the false positive.[1]

Now all these characteristics are the facts of the world we know. The logical errors which it is the aim of the treatise *On the Improvement of the Understanding* to remove have their origin in the corporeal imagination; and the corporeal imagination, with its faulty order, its false positive, its bad vocabulary, and misleading arguments, is the product of the buffetings upon man of the external universe of which he is physically a part. The necessary preliminary, therefore, to the discovery of truth, is to learn to distinguish between the true idea of the intellect as it works through its own activity, and the false ideas which arise from the passive acceptance of the external world. 'The true method', then, we find Spinoza writing to a zealous correspondent,[2] 'lies solely in the cognition of the pure intellect, in the acquisition of which it is *primarily necessary* to distinguish between *intellect and imagination*.'

§ 2. '*Imaginatio*' *and the Problem of Attributes in Spinoza*

Imagination is the lowest stage in human knowing, and at this stage knowledge so-called expresses itself in the form of the imaginational attribute. The atheist, as we saw, learned to deny God because 'he had not understood what was meant by God'. But these misunderstandings, which lead to the corrupt idea of God, are due to the corporeal imagination. Men apply their 'mutilated', 'inadequate', and 'partial' ideas to that which is beyond partial reasonings. 'They con-

[1] §§ 87–90 and 91 note. Cf. *Eth.* I, 15 sch.; II, 40, sch. I; II, 47 sch.; IV, 62 sch.; *Ep.* XII.

[2] *Ep.* XXXVII; cf. *Eth.* II, 49 sch. ('lectores moneo ut accurate distinguant inter ideam sive mentis conceptum et inter imagines rerum quas imaginamur').

found His intellect with that of man, and His power with the power of kings.' [1]

Spinoza, therefore, takes up the problem at the point where it was dropped by Maimonides. Maimonides had shown that no attribute drawn from human analogy could be applied to God; Spinoza, accepting the demonstration, seeks for attributes not derived from human analogy. To both thinkers it is the anthropomorphic description which is anathema and must be swept away; but whereas Maimonides stops with the bare affirmation of a positive essence, Spinoza seeks to determine the very nature of positiveness. 'The more attributes I attribute to any thing,' he writes to De Vries, 'the more I am compelled to attribute to it existence:' but hastens to add, 'that is to say, I conceive it more really,[2]—the opposite of which would be true if I were treating of a Chimaera.'

That this is the true history of the Spinozistic attribute may be seen by a study of its development in the Spinozistic text. The trend of the whole early discussion of attributes in the *Cogitata Metaphysica,* which, indeed, follows closely, often verbally, on Maimonides, is to show that if we retain them we must understand them in a way not drawn from human conceptions: God is one—but not in the sense of being one of a class; God is 'good'—but only by analogy and looking to our standards; God is 'living'—if by life we are content to understand nothing but His essence by which He persists.[3]

[1] *Cog. Met.* II, 3, § 7, and *Eth.* II, 3, sch.; cf. *Theol.-Pol.* VI, § 58, 'Omnes enim qui aliquantulum supra vulgum sapiunt, sciunt Deum non habere dextram &c. . . . Haec inquam ii sciunt qui res *ex perceptionibus puri intellectus* iudicant, *et non prout imaginatio a sensibus externis afficitur* ut vulgus solet quod *ideo* Deum corporeum et imperium regium tenentem imaginatur. . . .'

[2] 'Magis sub ratione veri.' *Ep.* IX, p. 34.

[3] *Cog. Met.* I, 6, § 2, § 7, § 10; II, 6, § 3; cf. *Guide*, e. g. I, 52, p. 71 ('even the term "existence" is applied to God and other beings homonymously'); 57, p. 80 ('The accident of unity is as inadmissible as the accident of plurality'). For the classification of *Cog. Met.* II, 11, §§ 3–4, cf. *Guide*. I, 53, p. 74 (above, p. 75). The very example of

Now, if we turn to the scholium of the seventeenth proposition of the first book of the *Ethics*, in which the conventional attributes of God come up again for consideration, the same general criticism is given, centring round the same use of the word ' attribute '. Any attribute drawn from human analogy must be disallowed with regard to God. It would seem, then, that we are faced again with the Maimonidean dilemma, and in our flight from error are driven into the arms of nothing.

This would be true if the imaginational were the only class of attribute possible. But, so Spinoza tells us, and that in his very earliest treatment of the question,[1] there is, as a fact, another class altogether. The attributes normally attributed by men to God are, as Maimonides saw, either ' extraneous denominations ' or ' descriptions of His activity '. But, apart from and beyond these classes, there is the ' proper ' attribute, ' through which we come to know Him as He is in Himself '. The application of the new doctrine is immediate and far-reaching, because it enables at once the positing of extension as an attribute of God. The well-known objections to this doctrine [2] are relevant only when extension is understood as the divisible and material corporeality of the *imagination*. We may, indeed must, concede, however, the admissibility of the *intellectual* conception of indivisible extension.[3]

a homonym employed in *Cog. Met.* II, 11, § 3 (' nec scientia Dei cum scientia humana magis convenit quam canis signum coeleste cum cane qui est animal latrans ') and repeated in *Eth.* I, 17 sch., is that given by Maimonides in his *Introduction to Logic*, cap. 13. [It would appear to have been conventional, cf. Steinschneider, *Hebräische Uebersetzungen*, p. 55, n. 68.]

[1] *Short Treatise*, I, cap. 2, pp. 30–31.

[2] *Guide*, I, 35, p. 50 ; II, Introduction, Prop. VII, p. 146.

[3] *S.T.*, p. 27 f. Cf. *Princ. Phil. Cart.* I, 9 sch. In *Ep.* XII and *Eth.* I, 15 sch. it is made clear that the cause of the misunderstanding is the substitution of the ' abstractions ' of the corporeal imagination for the pure ideas of the intellect : ' Si quis tamen iam quaerat, cur nos ex natura ita propensi simus ad dividendam quantitatem : ei

The imaginational attributes, then, go to make way for the intellectual—infinite in number, though two only are known to us; and Spinoza may well have considered himself safe from the charge of atheism which had been advanced against Maimonides for his denying human knowledge of God.[1] But it was not so. A God indescribable in imaginational terms will never be recognized by the majority of mankind. 'You say', writes his friend Boxel,[2] 'that you deny human attributes of God in order not to confuse the nature of God with that of man. So far, I approve. We do not perceive the way in which He wills and understands, considers, sees and hears. But if you deny categorically the existence of these activities and the validity of our highest thoughts of God, and affirm that they are not in God, even in the "eminent" and metaphysical sense; then I do not understand your God—*tuum Deum ignoro*—nor what you mean by the word.' And Spinoza can only point out, in reply, the old truth which he had learned from Maimonides: any imaginational attribute has significance only in relation to the ascriber; and there is no more objective reality in the human descriptions of God advanced by Boxel than there would be in a mathematical description given, say, by a triangle, if it happened to be articulate. An idea and an image are not the same. We cannot form an image of God, but we can have an intellectual idea of Him, howbeit incomplete.[3]

respondeo quod quantitas duobus modis a nobis concipitur, abstracte scilicet sive superficialiter, prout nempe ipsam *imaginamur*, vel ut substantia, quod a *solo intellectu* fit.'

[1] Cf. the quotation from Makrizi in Renan, *Averroès* [3], p. 42.

[2] *Ep.* LV, p. 198.

[3] *Ep.* LVI, p. 202; cf. *S.T.* II, cap. 22, p. 133: 'I do not say that we must know Him just as He is or adequately, for it is sufficient to us to know Him to some extent.'

§ 3. '*Imaginatio*' and the '*Deliverance of Man*' in *Spinoza*. '*Scientia intuitiva*' and *Immortality*

The passage to the intellectual idea of God is the theme of the *Ethics*. The servitude of man lies in the fact that he is necessarily a part of nature, and necessarily bound to imagination. The liberty of man lies in the fact that he can rid himself, to a certain extent, of imagination. The end of man is to know,[1] and knowledge proceeds through the negating of imaginational thought. The whole system of human standards—good and evil, right and wrong—are void of any absolute value, because they are drawn from human analogies based on human needs and experience; but if they are to have any meaning at all—and such meaning can only be relative to human life—we must set up some fixed standard of life by reference to which they may be secured some stability.[2] But since the aim of life is knowledge, our only absolute is the search for knowledge. All that helps to knowledge is good; all that stands in the way of knowledge, bad. Moral, as well as logical, defects are due to the fragmentary outlook. The only way to rid ourselves of them is to rise above the fragmentary outlook and attain a more comprehensive vision.[3]

The gradual growth of things from the imaginational 'point of view' into knowledge proceeds upwards through the generalizations of science, though it is not completed at

[1] *Eth.* II end; IV, 26, 28, 52 dems. and App., caps. 4–5.

[2] *Eth.* IV, pref.

[3] 'Vir fortis hoc apprime consideret, nempe quod omnia ex necessitate divinae naturae sequentur, ac proinde quicquid molestum et malum esse cogitat et quicquid praeterea impium, horrendum, iniustum et turpe videtur, ex eo oritur quod res ipsas perturbate mutilate et confuse concipit; et hac de causa apprime conatur res, ut in se sunt, concipere et verae cognitionis impedimenta amovere ut sunt odium, ira, invidia, irrisio, superbia, et reliqua huiusmodi.' IV, 73 sch. That the motive of the *Ethics* is the conception of morality as an 'applied logic' is the theme of M. Brunschvicg's volume on Spinoza.

that stage. The highest knowledge is not knowledge of a general law. As we have seen, knowledge *per essentiam rei* is knowledge of the individual. To understand as God understands we must proceed with the least possible abstraction, and try to apprehend the concrete actuality of the individual thing within the indivisible whole of Being.[1] Knowledge, therefore, is not the offspring of a union between imagination and thought. It is intellect alone which is the source of knowledge. Thought is different in kind from perception.[2] Thought is active, perception passive. Thought is not pictorial, and where you have a picture you have not thought.[3] We rise to thought, then, not through imaginational perception, but by ridding ourselves of imaginational perception. But to say that we 'rise to' thought is inaccurate. It is thought which comes down to us when we free the way by removing the misunderstandings from which we suffer through being inevitably a part of nature. It is indeed thought which comes to itself.[4]

[1] *D.I.E.* §§ 55, 75–6, and 93; *Eth.* II, 44 cor. II, dem. and V, 36 sch.; *S.T.* II, c. 6, p. 50 ('God, then, is the cause of and providence over particular things only'); and *Ep.* XIX, p. 67: 'Deus res non abstracte novit', with its obverse, 'Quo magis res singulares intelligimus eo magis Deum intelligimus.' (*Eth.* V, 24.) (Cf. Joachim, *Study*, pp. 264 ff.)

[2] *D.I.E.*, § 84; *Eth.* V, 28 and dem.

[3] *Eth.* II, 48 sch., 49 sch., second paragraph; II, def. 3 expl.; 43 sch.

[4] This account would seem to hold even of the *Short Treatise*, in spite of its well-known doctrine of the passivity of thought. The statement that knowledge is 'a direct revelation of the object itself to the understanding, not the consequence of something else, but immediate' (II, cap. 22, p. 133) is only an exaggerated way of expressing the (anti-Cartesian) idea that the will has no power to interfere with it (cf. Wolf's note, p. 221). And so Spinoza can write quite consistently in II. 15, of 'truth as revealing itself and also what is false' (p. 103); and, in the following chapter (p. 109), of the understanding as being 'passive, an awareness in the soul of the essence and existence of things, so that it is never we who affirm or deny something of a thing, but it is the thing itself that affirms or denies, in us, something of itself'. If thought and reality are the same, it makes little difference

By ridding himself of the passive imagination a man becomes more active and individual. The nature and duration, however, of the individuality so acquired must be carefully noted, because it would seem at first sight that it would be, from the point of view of the individual, loss of individuality. Indeed, Spinoza seems to go out of his way to deny the existence of an individual 'soul';[1] and in any case memory, the indispensable adjunct of personality as we understand it, is simply a physical phenomenon.[2] Yet the doctrine of degrees of reality, applicable ontologically, ethically, and psychologically,[3] suggests how differentiation within the whole may be conceived. The differentiation is conscious,[4] not, however, dependent on memory, but of the nature of an 'immediate feeling', which, in the highest degree, is the beatitude of perfection itself. In this state life is intellectual purely, the 'eyes of the mind' being the 'demonstrations themselves'.[5]

whether we speak in terms of the autonomy of the one or of the other.

[1] Man, like other things, is simply a 'balance of motion and rest', and liable to redistributions which appear to us as 'alternations of personality' or the phenomena of birth and death (*Short Treatise*, II, Pref. notes 8–10, pp. 63–4; *Eth.* IV, 39 and sch.).

[2] *Eth.* II, 18; V, 21.

[3] *Eth.* II, 13 sch.; *Ep.* XXIII, pp. 105–6: *Eth.* III, 57 sch.

[4] 'Vita et gaudium' = 'idea sive anima eiusdem individui', and differs in different men according to their 'essentia' (III, 57 sch.); but the 'essentia' has an eternal place in God (V, 22), in whom therefore 'sentimus experimurque nos aeternos esse' (V, 23 sch.).

[5] V, 23 sch.; cf. *Theol.-Pol.* XIII, § 17 ('res indivisibiles et quae solius mentis sunt objecta'—the reference is to God—'nullis aliis oculis videri possint quam per demonstrationes'). The possibility of pure memory, advanced by Descartes (*Letters*, vol. iii, p. 626) to meet the problem of survival of personality—'je trouve en nous une memoire intellectuelle qui est assurément indépendante du corps'—is not accepted in *D.I.E.* § 82 and § 83 note; and it would seem that Leibniz' criticism (*Réfutation Inédite*, p. 58), 'ratio sine imaginatione et memoria est consequentia sine praemissis', would be unescapable. Already, however, in *Eth.* II, 18 sch., in which memory is explained, it is made clear that the order of the intellect, which is distinct from physical

The highest type of knowledge, made way for by the removal of imagination, the 'eternal' knowledge, that is, which brings a timeless satisfaction to the mind, is the knowledge of things 'in God' as 'real or true'.[1] The more we learn to know things 'in God' the more we love Him, or, He loves Himself.[2] Only now can we understand the nature of the *scientia intuitiva*—it is the knowledge of God as God knows Himself, and in which we participate in proportion as we perceive our inherence in Him as Knower and Known.[3] 'Immortality' in the popular[4] sense has no meaning. Eternity, perfection, individuality, is independent of what we call 'this' life. In so far as a man rids himself of imagination or the partial point of view, he achieves his immortality. The *ordo ad intellectum* is; the *ordo ad naturam*, or the order of imagination, is not. The logical contrast between intellect and imagination pursues us even in the question of the final destiny of man.[5]

It is clear, then, from Spinoza's own words, and from a general consideration of his system as a whole, how fundamental to his thought is the conception of imagination. To it we owe his resolution of the logical problem of the nature of error; of the theological problem of the attributes of God; of

memory, is real. It is this 'order' which does not 'perish' with the body, because it has nothing to do with the body. 'Nam mens non minus res illas sentit quas intelligendo concipit quam quas in memoria habet.' *Eth.* V, 23 sch.

We have interesting testimony of Spinoza's conception in the record of a conversation between Tschirnhausen and Leibniz (ap. Stein, *Leibniz und Spinoza*, p. 283): 'Putat nos morientes plerorumque oblivisci et ea tantum retinere quae habemus cognitione quam ille vocat intuitivam quam pauci norint.'

[1] V, 27; 29 sch.; 33 sch.

[2] V, 32, and 36.

[3] V, 36 sch.; 38 dem. and sch.; 39 sch. It will be noted that the quantity of the 'immortal' part of mind depends on the amount of knowledge acquired.

[4] V, 41 sch.

[5] 'Pars mentis aeterna est intellectus per quem solum nos agere dicimur; illa autem quam perire ostendimus est ipsa imaginatio.' V, 40 cor. The word 'illaesa' in V, 38 dem. end, is significant.

the ethical problem of the aim of human life; and of the metaphysical problem of the soul and its immortality. Now if it be true, as has been asserted,[1] that 'in the Spinozistic philosophy there are few differences from Descartes which cannot be traced to the necessary development of Cartesian principles', we should expect to find the source of this fundamental idea in Descartes. But the most cursory examination of the ways in which Descartes treats these various problems shows at once that, whatever his solutions may be, they are not those of Spinoza. He recognizes that 'man is a part of nature', [2] but develops the doctrine in the physiological sense only. He seeks for the origin of error, but finds it in the indeterminism of man.[3] The religious opinions which he defended and considered it the chief merit of his philosophy that it enabled him to defend, were those of the dominant Church; [4] and he would seem to have contributed little to a positive theory of ethics beyond the apophthegm *bene vixit bene qui latuit*.[5] Since, however, the word *imaginatio* occurs often in

[1] By Edward Caird: article *Cartesianism* in *Encyclopaedia Britannica* (ed. XI, p. 121, col. 1), reprinted in vol. ii of his *Essays on Literature and Philosophy*, Maclehose, 1892.

[2] e. g. 'Superest adhuc una veritas cuius cognitio mihi videtur admodum utilis nempe quod . . . cogitare debeamus non posse quempiam per se solum subsistere et re vera *nos esse ex partibus Universi unam*, et potissimum unam ex Terrae partibus huius videlicet politiae, societatis, familiae, quicum domicilio sacramento nativitate conjuncti sumus; *Totius autem cuius pars sumus*, bonum privato bono debet anteponi; attamen cum modo et ratione,' &c. (*Ep.* I, 7, p. 16).

[3] Above, pp. 30–1; and Spinoza's criticism (*Ep.* II).

[4] Above, p. 28, n. 1.

[5] *Ep.* II, 76, p, 249 (to Mersenne). The point of cleavage between Descartes' 'Passions of the Soul' and the fourth book of the *Ethics* lies, as usual, in the conception of the power of the will. In Descartes' ethics, as in his logic, the will is supreme, and has absolute power over our emotions, a point of view against which the whole of Spinozism is one long protest, from the *Short Treatise* (e. g. II, cap. 5, p. 80, l. 8–18) to the *Tractatus Politici* (e. g. II, § 6; X, § 9). The very significant addition of Spinoza to his quotation (in *Eth.* V, pref.) from

his works, it will be worth while to trace its usage in some detail, in order to exhibit once again the characteristic peculiarity which makes our general problem so complex. For in this case, as in so many other cases, of apparent dependence of Spinoza on Descartes, the words really belong to and originate in the great Aristotelian tradition, and so are common to all post-Aristotelian thinkers; [1] the ideas, however, are not found in Descartes at all, but are found in their plainest and most avowed form in Maimonides.

§ 4. *The uses of 'Imaginatio' in Descartes*

To Descartes imagination is primarily a psychological fact. It is defined as the 'particular effort of mind' which calls up a mental picture, and which is distinguishable from intellection only by the object of its interest. 'In pure intellection the mind in some manner turns on itself, and considers some of the ideas which it possesses in itself; in imagining it turns towards its body and sees there something conforming to an idea which has been either intellected by it or perceived by the senses.' [2] When, however, Descartes, in the Treatise on the 'Passions of the Soul', [3] comes to investigate its psychological character more closely, he does not make it clear either what process is involved, or what are its determining conditions. If the object corresponding to the image may or may not be real; if in the calling up of the image the will may or may not be exercised; if in the framing of the image the 'animal spirits' may or may not pass through the proper channels; then it would seem that a scientific account

the 'Passions of the Soul' ('commotiones animae quae . . . *N.B.* producuntur'—see Van Vloten's editions) sums up the whole point n two letters.

[1] This is brought out very clearly in the essay of Prof. J. Guttmann, *Spinozas Zusammenhang mit dem Aristotelismus* in *Judaica Festschrift zu Hermann Cohen* (Cassirer, 1912), p. 516.

[2] *Med.* VI, p. 73: 14–20.

[3] Articles 19–12, 26.

of imagination is impossible. The crucial difficulty, however, occurs in the third Meditation, where the very existence of God is at stake. The word 'idea', we are told,[1] properly applies to thoughts which are 'as it were images of things [2] . . . thoughts such as those of a man, or a chimaera, the heavens, or an angel, or God'; and any idea or image in itself is just as true as any other. Imagining, therefore, would seem to be an essential function even of the 'pure' intellect, seeing that the very idea of God is only a thought in so far as it is an image.

This statement was seized on with avidity by his materialistic critics; Hobbes, in particular, being rejoiced to find confirmation of his suspicion that God was either corporeal or non-existent.[3] As often, Descartes' replies are not satisfactory or consistent with the original affirmation—a fact which would present matter for surprise were it not for the revelations of a letter to Clerselier. The obvious objection to the ontological argument, Descartes says, is that an idea might be held to comprehend a chimaera, and that, therefore, to admit the argument from idea to reality would involve admitting the reality of the chimaera.[4] Now the chimaera is a product not of 'intellect' but of 'imagination'. One way, therefore, of meeting the objection is to affirm that any idea, whether of the imagination or of the intellect, involves reality. For this reason, Descartes goes on to say, he brought together in the *Meditations* the product both of intellection and of imagination within the confines of the one word 'idea'. The existence of God and that of the chimaera now stand or fall together, and both God and the chimaera (the latter in a certain sense only) exist. Descartes, then, defends the argument for the existence of God by the device of admitting the reality of the

[1] *Med.* III, p. 37: 3–6. [2] 'Tanquam rerum imagines.'

[3] *Obj.* III, pp. 178–81, cf. the remarks of Gassendi (V, pp. 265–8 and 329). For Hobbes' materialistic doctrine of God see the passages collected in Lange, *History of Materialism*, Book I, Part III, cap. 2, last note. [4] Cf. Leibniz' comment above, p. 38, n. 2.

chimaera; and that is only effected by deliberately turning thought into an image, and allowing any image the validity of thought.[1]

If for dialectical purposes, however, Descartes is willing to confuse imagination with intellect, in his private correspondence he severs them completely. Here he acknowledges the inconclusiveness of the arguments of the *Discourse* for the existence of God, but excuses himself on the ground that 'judgements resting on the senses or imagination, not from pure intellect, are necessarily false or uncertain'.[2] But this confining of strict proof in metaphysics to the pure intellect, as opposed to the imagination, leads us to still greater difficulties when we remember the more technical use of the word. The one science which has achieved apodeictic certainty, and which is to be the model for all the sciences, including metaphysics, is precisely that science which without the aid of imagination would lose its peculiar character. The 'schematizing' imagination, as it was afterwards called, is for Descartes an essential factor in mathematical investigation, and yet it is precisely this same imagination which is the bane of metaphysics.[3] And this opposition between the imaginative and the speculative, which is none other than the opposition between

[1] 'Cum esset mihi animus argumentum pro Dei existentia ducere ex idea sive cogitatione quam de illo habemus, existimavi debere me primo distinguere nostras omnes cogitationes in certa quaedam genera ut observarem quaenam sint illa quae possunt decipere; atque *ostendendo vel ipsas chimaeras nullam in se habere falsitatem illorum opinioni irem obviam qui ratiocinationem meam repudiare possent, eo quod ideam quam de Deo habemus in numerum chimaerarum referant.*' *Ep.* I, 119, p. 381. For the Cartesian chimaera cf. above, p. 113.

[2] '. . . hanc materiam melius tractare non poteram, nisi fuse explicando falsitatem aut incertitudinem omnium iudiciorum a sensu aut imaginatione pendentium et deinde ostendendo quaenam sunt illa quae non pendent nisi ab intellectu puro et quam evidentia sint et certa.' (*Ep.* I, 112, p. 362, to Mersenne.)

[3] '. . . ea enim ingenii pars, imaginatio nempe, quae ad Mathesim maxime iuvat, plus nocet quam prodest ad Metaphysicas speculationes.' (*Ep.* II, 33, p. 130, to Mersenne.)

mathematics and metaphysics, comes out again most interestingly in the famous passage in which he describes his way of life: 'I spend only a very few hours a day', he writes, 'in those thoughts which exercise the imagination; and only a very few a year in those which exercise the pure intellect.' [1] Now 'the thoughts which exercise the imagination' are those which relate to mathematics; the 'thoughts which exercise the pure intellect' are those which relate to metaphysics.

It is, of course, true that all these various usages correspond to psychological facts, and some, indeed, were to find fruitful treatment at the hands of Descartes' successors. It is, however, important to note that they hold no integral part in the system, and vary in accordance rather with the needs of the moment than with any fundamental underlying conception. When we turn to Spinoza, we find precisely the opposite case. Imagination has a definite meaning with a definite place in the whole system. Introduced from its very heart, it is the instrument for the resolution of its primary difficulties, including, as we have seen, not only the logical problem of error and the ethical problem of evil, but the metaphysical problem of man's final end and immortality. To us it is natural to look to the pages of Maimonides for an explanation of this peculiar use. Since the principle on which it depends, that nature is one whole of which man is a part, is, as we saw, derived from Maimonides, it is not unnatural to suppose that the working out of the principle in the detail of its practical application is to be found in Maimonides as well.

[1] 'Et certe possum ingenue profiteri, praecipuam quam in studiis meis secutus sum regulam et quam puto mihi prae ceteris profuisse in cognitione nonnulla comparanda, fuisse, quod *paucissimas singulis diebus horas iis cogitationibus impenderem quae imaginationem exercent; per annum autem paucissimas iis quae intellectum solum*; reliquum vero tempus sensibus relaxandis et animi quieti dederim; imaginationis vero exercitiis annumero etiam colloquia seria, illudque omne quod attentionem poscit.' (*Ep.* I, 30, p. 62–3.)

§ 5. *The Grades of Natural Knowledge in Maimonides. 'Imaginatio' and the Problem of Error. Prophecy and 'Scientia Intuitiva'*

To Maimonides all things in the created universe are composed of 'matter' and 'form', the doctrine being saved from a dualism by the consideration that the distinction is not physical, but logical.[1] Man, being a part of the created universe, is also composed of matter and form. This fact is unsurmountable, and conditions all knowledge. Pure form or God cannot be known by man, because man, even the highest, retains a 'material' element. There are natural limits to human knowledge, because man cannot know anything beyond the material universe of which he is a part.[2]

The lowest stage in knowledge, if it can be called knowledge at all, is the perceptive knowledge of the ordinary man who is bound down to the immediate facts of his corporeal environment and the prejudices of convention. There are, however, two higher stages. The first is the stage of the scientist; the second, that is to say, the highest of all, is the stage of the prophet. In this doctrine the significance of the 'triplicity' of the *Guide* which we had occasion to note before,[3] stands revealed. The ordinary man (and with him the theologian); the scientist and Aristotelian philosopher (who is at war with the theologian); the prophet, who is one with the true metaphysician; are representatives of these three stages of knowledge. Each stage and each class has its opinions on all the great problems—the being of God; the origin of the universe; the structure of created things. These particular problems are discussed in the first portion of the *Guide*, and we have followed

[1] *Guide*, I, 72 (p. 114); II, 1 (p. 151); II, 17 (p. 180); III, 8 (p. 261). The fundamental character of this position has been shown by Dr. D. Neumarck in, e. g., *Toldoth Ha-Ikkarim*, vol. ii, cap. vii.

[2] *Guide*, I, caps. 31–4; cf. above, p. 94, n. 1.

[3] Above, p. 68.

them in their order and general outline. The second portion deals with the character of these stages themselves. The second half of the second book gives the general theory, under the name of the theory of prophecy ; while the third and last book is concerned with a discussion of its ethical consequences, in the course of which is given an apologia for the commandments of the Pentateuch, and a treatment of the problems of evil, providence, and the end of man. The *Guide*, then, presents a complete and homogeneous whole, and its central core is the theory of knowledge.

The key is supplied by an earlier chapter, that on God as the unity of *intellectus*, *intelligens*, and *intelligibile.*[1] Intellect, we learn, is nothing apart from that which it 'intellects' by its action ; and the 'intellected' is nothing apart from the action of the intellect. In God, who is intellect always in action, these two are identical with Himself. For, being pure intellect, He does not pass from 'potency' to 'actuality' as man does, but is always 'actual' ; His understanding, therefore, which is His essence, and the objects of His understanding, are one. The origins and destiny of this theory are well known,[2] but it is essential to note its specific limitations. The proposition is true only in the case of the purest intellection, which *ex hypothesi* is impossible to man. Man can only hope to enjoy it intermittently,[3] and that only when he achieves the severance of his thinking from 'the representative faculty—the reproduction of a material image in *imagination*'.[4]

For in direct contrast to the intellect stands the corporeal imagination : 'The intellect analyses and divides the component parts of things ; it forms abstract ideas of them ;

[1] I, 68.

[2] See the concluding page of Hegel's *Encyclopaedia*, where the famous passage in Book Λ of Aristotle's *Metaphysics* is transcribed as the last word of his own philosophy.

[3] *Guide*, Introduction, p. 3 (cf. Arist. *Metaph.* Λ, c. xi, § 7).

[4] I, 68, end, p. 102.

represents them in their true form as well as in their causal relations; . . . distinguishes that which is the property of the genus from that which is peculiar to the individual—and determines whether certain qualities of a thing are essential or non-essential. Imagination has none of these functions. It only perceives the individual, the compound in that aggregate condition in which it presents itself to the senses; or it combines things which exist separately, joins some of them together and represents them all as one body . . . Hence it is that some imagine a man with a horse's head, with wings, &c. This is called a fiction . . . it is a thing to which nothing in the actual world corresponds. Nor can imagination in any way obtain a purely immaterial image of an object . . . Imagination yields, therefore, no test for the reality of a thing. . .'

This interesting passage [1] goes on to give examples of things which, though impossible to the imagination, are yet intellectual truths; or which, though possible to the imagination, are in fact demonstrably fictions. Possibility is only another name, then, for compatibility with intellectual demands. That we cannot imagine such a phenomenon as that presented by the antipodes or by the results of certain mathematical theorems, has nothing at all to do with their real existence. Any argument, therefore, drawn from the imagination is to be rejected at once.

When we remember the place of this polemic, its importance is manifest. It occurs in the chapters devoted to the criticism of the Kalam, i. e., of the theological, or lowest, stage of human intelligence. That the whole theory is systematic and fundamental, not merely an *ad hoc* assumption, is evidenced by the

[1] I, 73, note to tenth Prop. (p. 130). Maimonides' special treatise on psychology, the so-called Eight Chapters, in which the points noted in the following pages receive systematic treatment, is available in Latin translations (e. g. in the *Porta Mosis* of Pococke) and in an English version by Gorfinkle (Columbia University Press, 1912). There is a monograph by Scheyer, *Das Psychologische System des Maimonides* (Frankfurt, 1845).

fact that it is woven into the whole texture of the *Guide*, a cursory examination of which shows how deeply the distinction has penetrated. If we look at the cases in which it comes into greatest prominence, it is interesting to observe that they all have reference to the nature of God. Thus it is the imagination that makes difficult the conceptions of the *incorporeality of God*, 'because those who do not distinguish between objects of the intellect and objects of the imagination' are unable 'to form a notion of anything immaterial'[1]; of the *simplicity of God*, because 'every existing material thing is necessarily imagined as a certain substance possessing several attributes'[2]; of the *complete infinity of God*, because 'with every additional positive assertion you follow your imagination and recede from the true knowledge of God'[3]; or, finally, of the *eternity of God*, the doctrine, that is, 'that there is no relation between God and time and space; for time is an accident connected with motion'[4] and therefore a part of the world of imagination.

It is, then, the imagination of man which stands in the way of his understanding of God; but that is only another way of saying that it stands in the way of knowledge. To say that the imagination cannot understand God, means, from the logical point of view, that it is unable to grapple with the nature of possibility. It is the imagination which is willing to accept any theory, 'whether the reality corresponds or not'; the imagination which, in order to substantiate its prejudices, will reject 'logical method' and 'demonstrated results'. It is, then, the intellect to which we must turn, and on which we must rely; and the mark of the intellect is precisely that it

[1] I, 49, p. 66; cf. I, 26, p. 35.
[2] I, 51, p. 69.
[3] I, 59, p. 84.
[4] I, 52, p. 71; II, 13, pp. 171–2. All these points reappear, of course, in Spinoza, cf. e. g. *Eth.* I, 8, 13, 15, and 33 sch. 2; II, 44 cor. II dem., 47 sch., and above, pp. 114 ff. *Ep.* XXXV gives an almost identical list, indivisibility being substituted for incorporeality.

possesses the power of understanding what law is, or, in Maimonides' phrase, the nature of the 'necessary, the possible and the impossible'.[1]

With this distinction in our minds, we are ready to be led to the third and highest type of knowledge. Of the three stages of mind, the prophetic, the scientific, and the imaginational, the first is a higher fusion of the other two, and combines organically the characteristics of both. Whereas imagination is individual and corporeal, and the intellect is universal and incorporeal, the prophetic 'conceives ideas which are confirmed by reality, and are as clear as if deduced by means of syllogisms'; it 'passes over intermediate causes' and 'draws inferences quickly' and is thus enabled 'to foretell a future event with such clearness as if it were a thing already perceived by the senses'.[2] Prophecy is therefore an immediate, super-inferential, and individual yet non-corporeal intuition, apprehending directly through essence, not indirectly by means of relations, and is the nearest approach of man to God, and of man's knowledge to God's knowledge. Through it man achieves the highest metaphysical truths, i. e., apprehends God 'as nearly as man can without becoming God'

In other words, Maimonides understands prophetic knowledge to partake of the *a priori* character of the knowledge of God, and therefore to be with it distinct in kind from the *a posteriori* knowledge of ordinary humanity, which, even in the higher stage represented by scientific thought, is still dependent on the empirical collection of data. This distinction is illustrated by an analogy drawn from the different knowledges of the workings of a clock possessed by the watchmaker and an external observer. In the one case, the working follows the knowledge, in the other the knowledge follows the working.[3] Whatever one may think of the idea as applied either to man or

[1] I, 73, note to tenth prop., pp. 130–1. Cf. (for Spinoza) above, p. 112.
[2] II, caps. 37–8; cap. 48, p. 249.
[3] III, cap. 21. Cf. Joel, *Lévi-ben-Gerson* (Breslau, 1862), pp. 56–7.

to God, and indeed it is common enough in the history of thought, it seems that we must recognize in it the source of the doctrine of *scientia intuitiva* in Spinoza. The *scientia intuitiva* is the reflection in the mind of the essence of a thing, as it manifests the essence of God who 'willed' it into being in accordance with His own nature. It, therefore, is God's knowledge, because His will and knowledge are identical with His essence. But such knowledge clearly cannot be discursive, proceeding from part to part, like our ordinary logical thought, still less fortuitous and fragmentary like the presentations of the imagination. It is an intuition of the part in its inherence in the whole.[1]

By prophecy, then, as by *scientia intuitiva*, things are seen in their essential natures. But the growth into Knowledge is not a phenomenon in vacuo. It involves for the knower an ascent in the scale of humanity. By knowing more and better, man becomes more characteristically man. We must turn, then, to the ethical consequences of this logical doctrine.

[1] Cf. 'Since God is a first cause of all other things . . . the *knowledge of God is and remains before the knowledge of all other things* . . .' *S.T.* II, 5, p. 81. 'Si intellectus ad divinam naturam pertinet, *non poterit uti noster intellectus posterior* (ut plerisque placet) vel simul natura esse cum rebus intellectis, quandoquidem Deus omnibus rebus prior est causalitate; sed contra veritas et formalis rerum essentia ideo talis est quia talis in Dei intellectu existit objective.' *Eth.* I, 17 sch. 'Hoc (= tertium) cognoscendi genus procedit *ab adaequata idea essentiae formalis quorundam Dei attributorum ad adaequatam cognitionem essentiae rerum.*' II, 40, sch. 2. The discursive character of human thought is due to its physical limitations: '*Omnia simul concipere res est longe supra humani intellectus vires*' (*D.I.E.*, § 102, cf. § 13).

§ 6. '*Imaginatio*' *and the* '*Deliverance of Man*' *in Maimonides. The Theory of Intellectual Immortality*

The process of training is described in the last chapters of the *Guide* under the heading 'How the perfect worship God': 'My son, so long as you are engaged in studying the mathematical sciences and logic, you belong to those who go round about the palace in search of the gate; . . . when you study physics you have entered the hall; and when after completing the study of natural philosophy you master metaphysics, you are in the innermost hall and are with the king in the same palace. You have attained the degree of the wise men who include men of different grades of perfection. . . . There are some who direct all their mind towards the attainment of perfection in metaphysics, devote themselves entirely to God . . . in the study of the universe. . . . These form the class of prophets.'[1] It will be noted that, in this passage, the 'natural' character of prophecy is clearly defined. The theory of prophecy is a theory of knowledge naturally acquired,[2] but the 'knowledge' is not at the intermediate, discursive level of logic, but at the ultimate, synoptic level of metaphysics. The first stage, that of imagination, is long since transcended.

If we ask what is the nature of the ascent from the point of view of logic, the answer is, through the removal of 'barriers' or 'screens' put into the way by the corporeal imagination.[3] The highest human wisdom is separated from the divine by at least one 'screen', that of corporeality, because so long as man is man he cannot but be liable to a minimum of corporeal

[1] III, cap. 51, p. 385.

[2] 'Ulterius erravit [Maimonides] circa prophetiam credens *hominem se posse sufficienter disponere ad gratiam prophetiae* et quod Deus non eligit in prophetando quemcumque hominem singularem sed illum qui se aptat ad talia; unde visus est velle divinam providentiam dependere ab operibus nostris.' (*De erroribus philosophorum*, XII, § 8.)

[3] III, cap. 9.

experience. It is only the very highest human wisdom, however, which is separated from God by one screen only. For all lower grades the screens are many, and increase in number the lower the grade. They take the forms of the positive fictions of the imagination, which can be dispelled only by the negations effected by the intellect. These positive fictions are of course nothing else but the attributes of the theologians; and it is only through the negative criticisms of the non-imaginational intellect that an approach is possible to the non-imaginable ideal.

With the attributes goes the problem of evil. Just as there is no absolute good, so there is no absolute evil. The error of the pessimists lies in their considering their own, or human troubles in general, as the centre of things. But man is a part of the universe, and therefore must be judged together with the whole of the universe. To give the verdict for pessimism on the evidence of personal sorrows is the supreme conceit of anthropocentricity.[1] Many things are evil to man, but man has no right to set himself up as the ultimate standard. The fundamental error of the imagination lies in its setting up of such 'final ends'. Teleological explanations, in the conventional sense at any rate, must be banned, because, like other values, they are personal and imaginative, and therefore untrue. The doctrine of the unity of nature must be accepted in the full and deep sense that 'the universe does not exist for man's sake, but each being exists for its own sake'[2]; and

[1] III, caps. 10–12. These passages became the subject of a battle-at-arms between Leibniz and Bayle. Cf. Theodicee III, Nr. 262–3, ap. Guttmann (*Moses ben Maimon*, vol. i, pp. 228–9).

[2] III, caps. 13–14, following on the discussion of evil, caps. 10–13. For Spinoza see *Eth.* I, App., and IV, pref. ('. . . ut . . . nullius finis causa existit, nullius etiam finis causa agit . . . Causa autem quae finalis dicitur nihil est praeter *ipsum humanum appetitum* . . .'). The opinion that 'Deum omnia propter hominem fecisse, hominem autem ut ipsum coleret' is derided by Maimonides (III, 13, p. 274) as well as by Spinoza (*Eth.* I, App., p. 217).

this doctrine carries with it the corollary for logic, that 'we must accommodate our opinions to things, not things to our opinions'.[1]

As if to emphasize the fact that the 'negations' must be made 'by proof' and not by 'mere words', i. e., that the 'revelation', though 'natural', and therefore not 'mystic' in the sentimental sense, is attainable only through the exercise of the logical faculty, Maimonides adds a final word. Throughout life 'it is the intellect which emanates from God unto us that is the link that joins us to God. You have it in your power to strengthen that bond, if you choose to do so, or to weaken it gradually till it break, if you prefer this. It will only become strong when you employ it in the love of God and seek that love. . . . When we have acquired a true knowledge of God, and rejoice in that knowledge in such a manner that whilst speaking with others or attending to our bodily wants, our mind is all that time with God; when we are with our heart constantly near God, even whilst our body is in the society of men; when we are in that state which the Song on the relation between God and man poetically describes in the following words: "I sleep, but my heart waketh; it is the voice of my beloved that knocketh"—then we have attained not only the height of ordinary prophets, but of Moses our teacher, of whom Scripture relates "and Moses alone shall come near before God . . ."'[2] It is through education in logic that character is acquired, and the character, once acquired, persists.

For knowledge is not a passive deposit, as it were, in the mind, but an active agent, influencing the character of the mind. To speak more accurately, it is only by becoming an active agent that the mind can acquire knowledge at all. God, as we have seen, is the unity of *intellectus*, *intelligens* and

[1] I, 71, p. 110, in the discussion of the Kalam, cf. Spinoza, e. g. *Ep.* XIII, p. 50 (a criticism of Descartes and Bacon), and *Theol.-Pol.* VI, § 34.

[2] III, 51, pp. 386–7.

intelligibile, and therefore in so far as man knows God, God may be said to know man, and, since 'divine Providence is connected with divine intellectual influence', to care for man. Except in the case of mankind, God's knowledge and care is not for the individual but for the type, but that is because the individual members of the type are not true individuals at all. Man, however, has it in his power to evolve individuality, and the greater the individuality attained (that is, the truer the ideas he achieves, or, the more his mind becomes that of God) the greater is the providence of God for him. God may be said to know or care for man in the exact proportion and degree in which man knows and cares for (or loves) God; therefore the knowledge and love of God for man and the knowledge and love of man for God are strictly commensurate terms. Indeed, they are almost interchangeable; because, 'when he does not meditate on God, when he is separated from God, then God is also separated from him'.[1]

This connexion between God and man is fixed at, and remains unaltered after, the death of the body. 'Their knowledge of God', we read, 'is strengthened when death approaches; their intellect remains then constantly *in the same condition*, since the obstacle is removed that at times had intervened between the intellect and the object of its action, and it continues for ever in that great delight.'[2] The 'absorption' in God which in life was commensurate with the amount of knowledge acquired of Him, continues unaltered and un-

[1] See the whole theory of Divine Providence, III, caps. 17–18. The important points are: 'Providence can only proceed from an intelligent being . . . those creatures therefore which receive part of that intellectual influence will become subject to the action of Providence in the same proportion as they are acted upon by the Intellect.' p. 288. 'Only individual beings have real existence, and individual beings are endowed with Divine Intellect; Divine Providence therefore acts upon these individual beings.' p. 290. Cf. the remarkable passage in III, cap. 51, pp. 388–9, containing the 'excellent idea' which occurred to him while writing.

[2] III, 51, p. 391.

interrupted after life. 'Immortality' depends on individuality, and individuality on knowledge; and knowledge is precisely the negating of the fictions of the imagination.

That this theory of 'intellectual immortality' [1] is strikingly similar to that of Spinoza is not a matter for surprise, seeing that it arises immediately from premisses which are common to both. The principal difficulty in the way of understanding it lies in the fact that since it is only the 'actualized' soul which persists, and since the 'actualized' soul is neither more nor less than the sum of acquired knowledge, it would seem that no differentiation is possible between the various actualized souls, the 'sum of knowledge' being presumably impersonal and the same for all alike. Even if we allow that mere 'demonstrations' [2] may be held to survive the physical mind in which they were achieved, we have yet to understand how the 'demonstrations' of one mind may be kept distinct from the 'demonstrations' of another. Memory, we are told, by Maimonides [3] as well as by Spinoza, may persist apart from the body; but how, one may well ask, can any one memory survive independently of any other?

The problem is made even more difficult if we remember the implications of the very conception of enumeration. Number and materiality are inseparable,[4] but the immortalized soul, particularly if equated with a 'sum of demonstrations', is nothing if not immaterial. It would seem that we are driven to some form of 'monopsychism', either in the psychological sense that the individual souls return to the one

[1] I am at a loss to understand why Joel (cf. Pollock, *Spinoza*, p. 271) thought it necessary to go to Gersonides for this thoery. See the excursus of Asher Crescas to his commentary on *Guide*, I, 70; Shem Tob on *Guide*, I, 74, arg. 7; and Euchel on *Guide*, II, Intr., prop. 16.

[2] Above p. 122 with n. 5.

[3] 'His learning remaineth with him,' goes a Talmudic saying, 'and he enjoys both this world and the world to come.' And Maimonides explains, 'In works on Metaphysics it has been shown that such knowledge, i. e., the perception of the Active Intellect, can never be forgotten. I, 62, pp 92–3.

[4] ὅσα ἀριθμῷ πολλά, ὕλην ἔχει, Arist. *Met.* Λ 8, § 18.

and undifferentiated world soul,[1] or in the logical sense that 'an adequate idea, when once thought, forms a permanent addition to the stock of scientific knowledge in the world'.[2]

The hint for a possible solution of the problem is given us in the sixteenth of the propositions of the philosophers which form the introduction to the second part of the *Guide*. Here we learn that 'purely spiritual beings, which are neither corporeal nor forces situated in corporeal objects, cannot be counted, *except when considered as causes and effects*'; and this same caveat is repeated in the three places in which the proposition is used.[3] The reason is clear. In the theory of the system of *natura naturata* developed by the Arabic philosophers on the basis of various passages of Aristotle, the Spheres which go to make up the descending scale of the planetary system have corresponding to them immaterial Intelligences, each one of which is derived from that immediately superior.[4] We must assume, therefore, as a fact of the created universe, that a causal series of differentiated spiritual beings is possible.

Now the lowest of these Intelligences is the Active Intellect which is operative in any effort of human thought, and with which rank the actualized souls of men.[5] We may, then, conceive of these souls being arranged in the same way as are the differentiated Intelligences, that is, in accordance with their degree of reality or of actualization (which depends, of course, on the quantitative sum of knowledge which they have acquired), and in relation to one another as causes to effects. This system of Intelligences running parallel with the system of material things (the whole being comprehended within the infinite and indivisible thought of the one God), is not very far

[1] Munk's note to *Guide*, I, 74, p. 434, n. 4.

[2] A. E. Taylor: 'The Concept of Immortality in Spinoza's *Ethics*', *Mind*, April 1896, p. 164.

[3] *Guide*, I, 74, p. 138; II, 1, p. 151; 4, p. 158.

[4] *Guide*, II, caps. 4–6. The sources are given in Munk, vol. ii, p. 51, n. 4, and in the second volume of Duhem's *Système du Monde*.

[5] *Guide*, II, cap. 4, p. 158.

removed, as Professor Pearson has reminded us, from the dual series in the universe presented to us in the metaphysic of Spinoza.[1] But the similarity becomes more striking still in its further consequences, for the conception that the actualized souls of men form, as it were, eternal links in the causal chain of Intelligences (a conception which Maimonides himself suggests only to reject) [2] does, as a fact, reappear in the scholium in which Spinoza sums up and concludes his doctrine of immortality: 'From this and from other propositions', he says, 'it is clear that our mind, in so far as it understands, is an eternal mode of thinking, which is determined by another mode of thinking, and this again by another, and so to infinity; so that they all together make up the eternal and infinite intellect of God.' [3]

That this state cannot be imagined is, of course, no argument against its existence, because it is avowedly the imagination which prevents man from comprehending the immaterial. And herein, from our immediate point of view, lies the most significant point of all. However we are to understand Maimonides' account of immortality (and the problem is intricate, and has given rise to much discussion), one point in it stands out as clearly as it does in the account given by Spinoza. Every man, so long as he thinks at all, is, in some, if an infinitesimal, degree, 'immortal', although compared

[1] In *Maimonides and Spinoza* (above, p. 102, n. 4), with reference to the cosmology of the *Strong Hand*. It will be noted that the motive of this strange theory is the fundamental assumption that 'the source of intellect must itself be pure intellect' (II, 4, p. 158), or 'that which produces form must itself be abstract form' (II, 12, p. 169). Cf. the second 'axiom of the philosophers', II, 22, p. 192: 'Things are not produced by other things at random; . . . a form cannot emanate from matter, nor matter from form.'

[2] 'That which remains of Zaid [after his death] is neither the cause nor the effect of that which is left of Amir.' I, 74, p. 138. The doctrine, however, seems to be accepted, though somewhat obscurely, in the earlier *Strong Hand*, I, 2, §§ 3–6, 4, §§ 8–9; V, 8, §§ 2–3.

[3] *Eth.* V, 40 sch.; cf. Joachim: *Study*, p. 309.

with the metaphysician, the completely uninstructed is 'like the beasts that perish'. The greater the place allowed to the imagination, the less is left to the intellect, and the smaller is the sum of knowledge acquired; the smaller the sum of knowledge acquired, the less is the degree of individuality attained, and the lower is the grade achieved in eternity; but whether the grade achieved be high or low, it is achieved in and during this life, and through the throwing off of the trammels of the imagination.

With the doctrine of intellectual immortality we may leave this peculiar though highly suggestive theory. Whatever may be thought of its intrinsic value, it sets the coping stone on our general thesis. To meet the one fundamental problem of all systems of philosophy Spinoza specifically rejected the solution offered by Descartes and adopted that offered by Maimonides. The account of reality given by Spinoza and Maimonides we saw earlier to be the same, but any account of reality is incomplete without an account of appearance. A theory of truth cannot stand without a theory of error; a theory of good without a theory of evil; a theory of the infinite without a theory of the finite. This integral portion of any coherent account of the universe, in its characteristic form, in the face of similar opponents, and with the same implications in every field of human speculation, we now see to have been taken over verbally by Spinoza from Maimonides. '*Praeclare distinguit Maimonides*', we may well then agree with Leibniz, '*inter intellectionem et imaginationem*'.[1]

[1] Curiously enough, this is Leibniz' final note to the *Guide*.

CONCLUSION

WITH this striking instance of detail our study comes to a close. Enough has been said to indicate the necessity of revising the conventional judgement that there was one unitary development in European philosophy from Descartes, through Spinoza and Leibniz, to Kant. Descartes and Spinoza represent two distinct poles of thought, examples of which may be found in every age. That the characteristic doctrine of Descartes was enunciated many centuries before by the Arabic theologians seems to be due not to a mechanical transference of ideas, but to an identity of intellectual needs. But be that as it may, the essential conflict between Descartes and Spinoza is found already clearly and definitely developed in the *Guide for the Perplexed*, and where Spinoza rejected the lead of Descartes, he not only followed that of Maimonides, but based his rejection on Maimonides' arguments, often, indeed, on his very words. 'A vast amount of learning and ingenuity', writes Principal Caird,[1] 'has been expended on the question of Spinoza's supposed obligations to Maimonides, Chasdai Crescas, and other distinguished philosophic writers of his own race . . .' but 'their occasional coincidences are such only to the ear.' In the light of the foregoing it seems clear that the 'supposed obligations' are something more than 'occasional coincidences'; and if we throw our minds back over the course which we have followed, we will appreciate how integral a place they occupy in the totality of Spinozism. We have watched the monism of Spinoza grow in the various stages of its natural development, and traced them back one by one to their analogue or origin in Maimonides. In some cases the principles involved are patent to the most casual reader; in others they are concealed by the historic termino-

[1] *Spinoza*, pp. 60, 69, (ed. 1910). Many similar judgements might be collected, cf. e. g. Pollock, *op. cit.*, p. 88; Kuno Fischer, *op. cit.*, p. 262 f.; Dilthey, *op. cit.*, p. 442.

logy in which they are expressed. All can understand the significance of the doctrine of the omnipresence of law in the organic unity of nature ; few see in the discussions anent the attributes of God the philosophical principle of relativity, or in the theory of the different grades of knowledge the essential basis of any monistic metaphysic. But whether the issues at stake are clear to the modern reader or not, Maimonides and Spinoza speak throughout with one voice.

My aim in this essay has been historical in a somewhat narrow sense and will have been realized if I have been enabled to set these giants of thought in their true connexion with one another. I may be permitted, however, to add a word with regard to the wider interest and significance of the argument. The position of Spinoza in the history of European thought is, it is generally acknowledged, peculiar. Neglected, except for purposes of execration, during his own lifetime and the following century, his work first met with recognition, howbeit over-extravagant, in the circles of the post-Kantian idealists, and had to wait for the last fifty years to gain its proper appreciation. This remarkable fact, which has prompted at least one historian of the problems of philosophy to treat of Spinoza after Kant, seems to stand in need of some special explanation. We cannot understand the historical place of a thinker, as M. Duhem reminds us,[1] unless we can determine not only his 'reading' but also his 'readers'; and in the case of Spinoza we have to account for the fact that his 'readers' were very few until a century and a half had elapsed after his death. In the light of the account which I have given it may be suggested that the Cartesian tradition had to reach its culmination in Kant before Spinoza could be 'read'; just as the attitude which he maintained in its regard was due to the work which he had early 'read' himself. Until Kant had worked out the logic of the pluralistic individualism of

[1] *Études sur Léonard de Vinci*, vol. i (Paris, 1906), Préf. pp. 6–7.

Descartes there was no room for the monism of Spinoza; and the monism of Spinoza is a direct derivative of the characteristic form which the monotheistic idea, in opposition to the current mythological pluralism, had assumed in the mind of Maimonides. The *Guide for the Perplexed*, therefore, is the key not only to the growth of Spinoza's system in Spinoza's own mind, comprising as it does both his own positive philosophy and the grounds of its opposition to and rejection of Cartesianism, but also to the peculiar history of the influence which it exerted upon the course of European speculation. The long line of thinkers who from Albert and Aquinas drew consciously and directly from the inspiration of the *Guide*, are succeeded by all those who during the past century have drunk from the well of Hegel.

INDEX